GRENADA GRINDER

This book is as factual as personal experience, extensive research, and interviews with participants will allow. Any errors are unintended, and the author apologizes for any omissions or errors.

Copyright © 2011 by Michael J. Couvillon

All pictures are used with permission.

Cover and design by Mark Babcock

Printed in the United States of America

Published by Deeds Publishing, Marietta, GA

First Edition, January 2011

For information on quantity discounts for promotional or premium use, write Deeds Publishing, PO Box 682212, Marietta, GA 30068 or www.deedspublishing.com

ISBN 978-0-9826180-8-0

GRENADA GRINDER

THE COMPLETE STORY OF AC-130H SPECTRE GUNSHIPS IN OPERATION URGENT FURY

BY MAJOR MICHAEL J. COUVILLON, USAF (RET.)

WWW.DEEDSPUBLISHING.COM

DEDICATION

To all current and former AC-130 Gunship crewmembers
Sierra Hotel!

"If you ain't Spectre, you ain't shit!"

(The Spectre logo is a Trademark of the Spectre Association)

IN MEMORIAM

SMSgt Paul G. Buege, Sensor Operator, Crew of Lima 59
KIA 31 Jan 91, Crew of Spirit 03, Kuwait

TSgt Robert L. Daniel, Aerial Gunner, Crew of Lima 60
KIA 14 Mar 94, Crew of Jockey 14, Somalia

MSgt Roy S. Duncan, Illuminator Operator, Crew of Lima 56
KIA 14 Mar 94, Crew of Jockey 14, Somalia

SMSgt Clyde C. Gowdy, Illuminator Operator, Crew of Lima 61
Died 29 Aug 07, Ft Walton Beach FL

TSgt Richard K. Smith, Aerial Gunner, Crew of Lima 58
Died 1984, Ft Walton Beach FL

Lt Col Paul C. Wonderly, Fire Control Officer, Crew of Lima 56
Died 29 Jan 09, Ft Walton Beach FL

CONTENTS

FOREWORD

In October 1983, foreign policy issues were front and center on the pages of America's newspapers almost every single day. Communist (Soviet) subversion activities were on-going in Central America and the Caribbean as well as in Southern Africa and other important regions of the world. Nuclear weapons and arms control were also hot issues at that time. The Cold War was anything but cold.

I had the privilege of serving as a Special Assistant for National Security Affairs to President Reagan at that time and it seemed as though foreign policy problems were almost overwhelming. The Reagan defense buildup was moving forward and the dangers of confrontation with the Soviet Union were generating genuine angst in the Congress and among the public.

President Reagan briefs Congressional Leaders on the Grenada Operation at 8 am meeting at the White House October 25, 1983.
Foreground, left to right: Congressman Bob Michel, Speaker Tip O'Neill, President Reagan, Senator Howard Baker; background left to right: Special Assistant to the President Christopher Lehman, and White House legislative staff Nancy Kennedy, M.B. Oglesby and Pamela Turner

It was in that environment that a new crisis began to emerge in the little noticed eastern Caribbean island of Grenada. In 1979, left-wing rebels (funded covertly by Cuba and the Soviet Union) launched an armed revolution and overthrew the government, establishing a new Peoples Revolutionary Government. In early 1983, there was increasing instability within the country and on October 13th Deputy Prime Minister Bernard Coard seized power, placing Prime Minister Bishop under house arrest.

Mass protests erupted and Prime Minister Bishop escaped from house arrest and tried to reassert his authority. Within days, Bishop was recaptured and executed along with several government officials loyal to him. That was followed by the Chief of the Grenada Army stepping in and forming a military council to rule the country.

The on-going subversion in Grenada and its implications for further subversion in the region were of great concern to President Reagan and his foreign policy advisors. The continuing presence of hundreds of Cuban "construction workers" (who were actually a detachment of Cuban Special Forces) combined with hundreds of "advisors" from the Soviet Union, East Germany, Libya and other pro-Soviet countries made it clear to many of us in the government that what was happening in Grenada needed to be stopped.

The issue came to a head very quickly when it appeared likely that the new revolutionary forces were intending to take hostage the American medical students at the Saint George's University. In President Reagan's view, that just wasn't going to happen if he could do anything about it – and he could and he did!

At a meeting in the Situation Room in the basement of the White House on October 22nd, the President assembled his senior national security advisors, including the Vice President, the Secretary of Defense, the Chairman of the Joint Chiefs, the Secretary of State, the Assistant Secretary of State for Latin America, the Director of the CIA, the National Security Advisor and a few senior staff from the National Security Council (of which I was one).

After hearing the views of his advisors, President Reagan decided that the United States needed to intervene. He said, "...we are going in!" The President directed the Chairman of the Joint Chiefs to be back at the White house with a plan the next day.

As is often said, the rest is history. However, prior to this book being written, the history of *Operation Urgent Fury* was incomplete. The "big picture" facts of the military operation were covered in the news media at the time with attention paid to the Army Rangers assault on the Point Salines Airfield, the combined Army Ranger, Army DELTA Force and Navy SEAL assault on Richmond Hill Prison, and the Navy SEALs rescue of Queen Elizabeth's Special Representative on Grenada capturing most of the attention. However, in most of the writings since that operation, the key role that was played by the AC-130H Spectre gunships has received barely a mention and yet, it was the enormous, timely and accurate firepower of these powerful aircraft that allowed the mission to be completed successfully.

As the mission unfolded in the early morning hours of 25 October, I was able to follow the progress of the operation from a White House communication facility as reports of the Special Operations Forces assaulted the Point Salinas Airfield. The operation launched at 5 am and it quickly became evident that the assault of the airfield was not going to be a "cakewalk." The so-called Cuban construction workers turned out (as anticipated) to be seasoned special forces and the airfield was well-defended with anti-aircraft weapons. It was here that the AC-130H Spectres first came into action. The three gunships that had been orbiting over the airfield (the crews of Couvillon, Sims, and Twiford) rolled in and quickly eliminated the anti-aircraft gun positions and also a good number of the Cuban Special Forces defenders of the airfield, thereby allowing the airborne troops to be dropped in a less hostile environment. These massive firepower gunships saved the day and saved many American lives that day.

Major Couvillon tells a spellbinding story of the critical role that AC-130H gunships played in the Grenada Operation -- from the short notice alert that their aircraft were going on a mission to "somewhere," through the whole operation from loading extra ammunition to firing in support of U.S. and coalition troops on the ground; to the White House Ceremony just a week after the operation ended celebrating the safe return of the medical students to the United States. President Reagan wanted to thank all of the U.S. military forces that had participated in the Grenada operation and he did so with enthusiasm on the South Lawn of the White House on a sunny November 7th.

I have been pleased to have stayed in touch with Major Couvillon all these years since the 1983 operation and I am very pleased that he has written the definitive history of the AC-130H Spectre in *Operation Urgent Fury*. It is a great read, full of interesting details that have not made it to the pages of history until now.

Just a few short weeks after the Grenada Operation, I had the privilege of flying a training mission in an AC-130H Spectre flying out of Howard Air Force Base in Panama and, to this day, I have treasured the 40 mm shell casings that resulted from some practice firing from "our" aircraft.

The readers of this book will feel as though they were on-board the aircraft for all of the missions as Major Couvillon has woven a gripping story that needs to be told.

To Major Couvillon and all the AC-130H crews that flew in support of *Operation Urgent Fury* I give my thanks for a job well done!

CHRISTOPHER M. LEHMAN
Former Special Assistant to President Reagan
November, 2010

ABOUT THE AUTHOR

Major Couvillon was commissioned through the AFROTC program at Louisiana State University in 1963, and graduated from Undergraduate Pilot Training at Williams AFB, AZ, in 1964. Over his 20 year flying career he flew the T-37, T-38, T-39, C-118, C-130B/E/H, and AC-130H aircraft, logging almost 6000 hours total, with over 5000 hours in the C-130 type aircraft.

He is a highly decorated Vietnam veteran with almost 600 combat hours in the C-130E and AC-130H, and holds the Distinguished Flying Cross, the Air Medal with seven Oak Leaf Clusters, and many other ribbons and awards. He first flew into Vietnam in 1965 and flew extensively in the combat zone as a C-130E Instructor Pilot in 1967-68. He was awarded the Command Pilot rating in 1979.

Figure 2. Maj Couvillon standing by #1 20mm gun

For many years he was an FAA Certified Flight Instructor (CFI), and still holds an FAA certificate with ratings in Single and Multi-engine aircraft with Instrument Rating, and holds Type Ratings for the civilian commercial versions of all the military transport aircraft he has flown.

He is co-holder of the previous C-130 endurance record of 29.7 hours when deployed non-stop as leader of a two-ship formation with four air refuelings from Hurlburt Field, FL to Andersen AFB, Guam, in 1979. The flight was a prelude to the Iran hostage rescue attempt in 1980.

At the time of the Grenada mission in October 1983 he was the senior Instructor Pilot in the 16th Special Operations Squadron, 1st Special Operations Wing, at Hurlburt Field, FL, having flown the gunships since 1978. (The accompanying photo was taken next to one of his unit's AC-130H Spectre gunships at Charleston AFB, SC, while TDY on Exercise Demo III about a week before deployment on Operation Urgent Fury.)

He retired from the USAF with 20+ years of service effective 1 March 1984, and after two years working in the burgeoning retail computer business, was employed in Civil Service as a Mechanical Engineer at the Air Force Research Laboratory Munitions Directorate at Eglin AFB, FL. In late 2004 after over 19 years of service, he retired for the second and last time in the grade of DR-III Senior Engineer (equivalent to GS-14).

Major Couvillon now resides with his wife of 49 years in Fort Walton Beach, FL, and enjoys each day working on projects in his many areas of interest. He has four grown children and seven grandchildren, some residing locally and others living within visiting distance in southern metropolitan areas. He is a Life Member of the Fraternal Order of Daedalians for military pilots, and a Charter Member of Seagull Flight #61. Volabamus. Volamus.

PREFACE

OVERVIEW OF HOW THE BOOK CAME TO BE WRITTEN

In October 1983 while serving as an AC-130H Spectre Gunship instructor pilot, I was ordered to participate in Operation Urgent Fury on one of six aircrews from my squadron. The operation's objectives were threefold: 1) to assure the safety of American citizens on Grenada, 2) the restoration of a democratic government in Grenada, and 3) the elimination of current and future Cuban intervention in Grenada.

In 2007, after having been retired from the Air Force for almost 24 years, I quite accidentally found a library book on Operation Urgent Fury that listed me by name as a principal participant. Not only did the book briefly recount some of my "daring" exploits, albeit with errors here and there and missing a few facts, it gave a very good description of the entire operation as I knew it. and a whole lot more about it that I didn't.

Although the author of the book described the gunship's contributing role in part as he told the larger story, the important details of the gunship's operation from my viewpoint were not included. These were the "behind the scenes" part. The gunship aircrews had been well trained to perform every task the mission required, but in this case it would require a series of events to go just right. As it actually happened, the gunships gave more than a good accounting of themselves from start to finish and that is the story that needs telling.

During the next few months after finding that book, with my interest piqued, I searched the library and the internet for more information on Urgent Fury, and found less (about the gunships) rather than more, so to speak. Mostly the story was told as "the gunships were there and saved the day," end of story. Some books didn't even mention Grenada in their list of conflicts, and some covered the operation but neglected to mention that the AC-130H gunships were even there. One report written about Operation Urgent Fury for the Joint Chiefs of Staff did not even mention Air Force gunships until almost the last page, and then mistakenly credited Navy A-7s and Marine helicopter gunships throughout the document for all the good things that happened by air-to-ground supporting fires. That was just about the last straw!

I did find a lot of specialty books about other service's Special Operations groups that also participated, like the Navy's Sea-Air-Land (SEAL) unit that had assigned assault missions, and the Army Special Forces helicopter units that flew them to their objectives. Another excellent publication, the Praetorian Starship, was written by my longtime friend retired Colonel Jerry Thigpen, a member of the 8th Special Operations Squadron, the gunship's sister unit at Hurlburt Field, FL that flew the MC-130H Combat Talon. The Talons led the airdrop of the Army Ranger Battalions on the primary objective airfield, Point Salines. Other works are about the U.S. Navy and the carrier led Task Force, and the Marines' role in seizing the northern part of the island.

The constantly missing theme was the complete and accurate story of the Spectre gunships and the details of their participation.

THE BOOK'S INTENDED PURPOSE

The purpose of this book is to fill that void and tell the complete story of the AC-130H Spectre gunship's role in Operation Urgent Fury, from the day the unit was alerted until after the last hurrah. Surprisingly, that period for the gunship was only 19 days, from 21 Oct 1983 until 8 Nov 1983.

There is one other obligation that I felt in writing this story, and that is to place the role of the AC-130 gunship in its rightful place in history. Although in terms of size and duration, the story of Grenada is but a small piece in the history of the United States Air Force, it is nonetheless an important one. As several historians have pointed out, it was the gunship's first time out since Vietnam, and it provided a milestone and valuable clues about what good or bad was happening to the gunships in the area of joint operations.

One of the most surprising things I learned during the research for the book is that very little that has been written about the Air Force mission in Grenada is now publicly available. After 27 years and in spite of my numerous requests using the Freedom of Information Act, a lot of the After Action reports from participating units and interviews with commanders and general officers at every level remain classified. Some Major Commands and Joint Commands of the day, or their successors, didn't respond to my FOIA requests as you might think they should. As of this writing I still had several open requests that had been active for more than three years.

Since Urgent Fury was almost totally a Special Operations show, the tactical and strategic airlift and the tanker communities have written very little although they played very important parts. The unclassified data to be found about them is mostly the statistics of how many sorties or hours they flew, or how many passengers or tons of cargo they carried.

TO WHAT EXTENT DOES THIS BOOK COVER THE TOPIC

Most of the Operation Urgent Fury books and documents also cover the political story of upheaval and revolution that occurred in Grenada during the months preceding the invasion. Several works that most aptly tell that story are available to the reader and listed in the bibliography. Although very interesting, I consider that story to be outside the intended scope of this book.

With that exception, this book totally covers every facet of AC-130H participation in Operation Urgent Fury from beginning to end. In addition to the author's personal experiences in the operation, it includes the formal and personal accounts of other crews in addition to the now de-classified crew mission debriefs recorded for use in official Air Force classified operational reports.

I decided early-on while writing the book that I wanted to tell more about the AC-130H gunship rather than less. Accordingly I have spared little detail and you will find plenty of it from crew, to airplane, to weapons, to ammunition, to operating procedures. I have also included descriptions of the flight tests that significantly enhanced the gunship capabilities in the sections on firing with external tanks and air refueling from the KC-10. Not to be left out because I thought it was important to the story, I have also included some of the interface between the gunships and the EC-130E Airborne Battlefield Command and Control Center (ABCCC) aircraft, and a brief story of their combat history and retirement from service.

And lastly, please know that I have spent countless hours in contacting and interviewing a cross section of the crew members who participated, in-person with a lot of them who still reside locally and the rest by e-mail and telephone. The accounts of what they remembered provided the glue for me to put the story together and to help me get it straight. It was a pleasure to work with them again, some I had not seen or talked with in 25 years.

ACKNOWLEDGMENTS

I would like to acknowledge a lot of folks and thank them for their help:

My special thanks first and foremost to my wife and family who tolerated my long hours of working only on the book, and who put up with my non-social moods. I plan to get back to a normal life just as soon as I've wrapped this thing up, I promise!

To Mark Adkin for writing the book "Urgent Fury: The Battle for Grenada" which was my bible and by far the most authoritative source on the subject.

To good friend Rich Davis for proof reading and providing the first sanity check on the original manuscript.

To Joe Caver at the Air Force Historical Research Agency (AFHRA) for helping me to unravel some of the Freedom of Information Act (FOIA) issues.

To friends Morgan & Tom Flach for performing research at the Ronald Reagan Presidential Library in Simi Valley, CA.

To folks that were very helpful in providing insights into the accounts of organizations that interfaced with the gunships during the combat operations: Bucky Burruss, Bruce Fister, Bob Gormly, Bob Johnson, Mike Matt, Jim Roper, Jim Schenk, and Jerry Thigpen.

AC-130H OPERATIONS

Special thanks to Dave Sims and Robb Schmitt for the mission materials, especially for the crew lists and maps. Also thanks to: Roger Betterelli (to whom I sent the 1st probing e-mail on 8 May 2003), Ron Broyles, Al Collette, Dick Dougherty, Gene Eller, Glenn Gaudette, Milo Gavin, Clyde Gowdy (now deceased), Don Kemper, Kirby Locklear (also for providing the awards information), Robbie Robertson, Paul Singleton, Larry Strelau, Bill Terry, Clem Twiford, Bob Wenger, Paul Wonderly (now deceased), Jerry Andersen, PJ Cook, and Bill Walter.

AIRBORNE BATTLEFIELD COMMAND AND CONTROL CENTER (ABCCC) OPERATIONS

Special thanks to Francis Mitchell and Aubrey McEachern for help with details on ABCCC operations, and especially the substitute crew lists. Also thanks to: Jonathan Bickel, Kevin Britt, Kenny Clower, Dana Cramer, Mark Doiron, Eddie Driggers, Keith Ellis, Jules Ferreira, Brian Garner, Gene Hilsheimer, Ray Hudgens, Stephen Ladd, Mike Mahoney, Michael Mekanik, Eric Morin, Mike Morris, Brian Muirhead, Bob Nelson, Norm Potter, Chris Robinson, Ray Roddy, Robert Schmidt, Robert Sheehan, Ken Sparks, David Volz, Don Watkins, Leonard Winston, and Ken Witkin.

PILOT IS IN THE SIGHT
ARM THE GUN!

Figure 3. This AC-130H Spectre Gunship is ready for business!

INTRODUCTION

Grenada Grinder closely follows the chronology of Operation Urgent Fury as we lived it from the beginning on 21 Oct 1983 to the end on 2 Nov 1983. Using the track of our crew's mission activities, I tell the story by describing events from our actual combat profile. These events are grouped into the first three chapters: *1) Pre-mission, 2) Day One,* and *3) Day Two & Mop Up.*

Along the way I explain in detail the employment of the complex AC-130H Spectre gunship weapon system. The weapon system itself is the real star of this story, and that will become evident as you read along. The secondary objective throughout is to give insight into how the crews make the system work, and how the system delivers its unbelievable firepower with such pinpoint accuracy.

CHAPTER 1   PRE-MISSION

The opening chapter begins by describing the crew's ground activities as we get ready to fly the mission. These are covered in sections titled **Squadron Alert and Recall**, and **Mission Briefing**. Most of the preparations for this mission are as normal as they would be for any standard live fire training mission, just with a lot more attention and excitement.

Next, I depart from the normal crew sequence of events by inserting information that is only available now in retrospect. With this perspective, the reader will be well informed and can understand the problems and situations as they come up later in the narrative. These sections are titled **Unplanned Contingencies**, and **The Intelligence Briefing**. It is essential to cover these items before the flight begins with the takeoff that occurs in Chapter Two.

And lastly, there are two tables in this chapter that add dimension to the ground threats we would face. They are titled **Anti-Aircraft Artillery (AAA) on Grenada**, and **They Knew**

We were Coming. Both posed hazardous conditions to our operation, each different in nature and timing.

CHAPTER 2 DAY ONE

Chapter 2 contains most of the mission's crucial employment events. It covers roughly the 24-hour time span from pre-takeoff on Monday afternoon, 24 Oct 1983, to mission recovery at Barbados on Tuesday, 25 Oct 1983.

Again it follows our actual sequence of events and includes: *At the Aircraft, Takeoff from Hurlburt, Enroute Air Refuel, Reconnoiter the Point Salines Runway*, the diversion of *Fort Jeudy*, and the live-fire Ranger support in *Come Running to Point Salines.*

Next the flight takes necessary time away from the action for the *KC-10 Air Refuel*, and then returns and continues live-fire at *Little Havana, Fort Rupert*, and the *Governor General's residence*. The chapter winds up with *Bingo Fuel* recovery at Roosevelt Roads, Puerto Rico, and the subsequent repositioning sortie in *Arrive Barbados*. Interspersed after the Fort Rupert event was the time wasting event of *Search for Richmond Hill Prison*.

CHAPTER 3 DAY TWO & MOP UP

The chapter begins with the introduction of the *Airborne Battlefield Command & Control Center (ABCCC)* aircraft and their interface with the gunships, including their shared maintenance effort, and the MC-130 Talons. Here we also visit the Joint Special Operations Command (JSOC) command structure aboard ABCCC. We then resume our operational missions with our last live fire at *Grand Anse Beach,* then continue with *Uncontrolled A-7s, Capture of General Hudson Austin,* and *Move to Roosevelt Roads.* Finally the somewhat amusing *Naming the Grinder* and *O'Club with A-10 Pilots,* and then we close out the mission with *Return Flight to Hurlburt.*

CHAPTER 4   POST MISSION

Chapter 4 covers my personal experiences in conjunction with non-flying post mission activities from 2–7 Nov 1983. I was very fortunate to be selected to attend President Reagan's White House reception as one of only ten representatives for all of the Air Force units that participated in Operation Urgent Fury. These events are described in *Invitation to the White House, Meet at the Pentagon, Arrive at the White House,* and *White House Ceremony on the South Lawn.* The chapter then closes with the *Air Force Times Interview* and the dreaded *Hurlburt Press Conference.*

CHAPTER 5   MISSION SCENARIOS AND TIME LINES: LIMA 57 THRU LIMA 61

Two other gunships flew similar missions (and share the limelight) along with the *Grenada Grinder* on Day-1, and my crew's story line describes our paths crossing during the day. In the fifth chapter, however, I have included individual standalone sections for the mission scenario and time line of each of those two aircraft and also for the three additional gunships that began arriving in the theater in the early hours of Day-2. This additional chapter completes the record for those five crews to the extent their stories are known.

APPENDICES

Appendix A - AC-130H Gunship Primer: What you need to know to understand gunship operations - Unless the reader is already familiar with gunship jargon and terminology, and has a working familiarity with gunship operations, it is recommended to first review this appendix. The primer will get you up to speed on at least the basic level of understanding that is needed to follow along on operation of the gunship. After reading the primer's comprehensive descriptions of crew operations, aircraft systems, and operational procedures, etc., a section entitled "Typical Target Attack Scenario" will pull it all together in a step-by-step 105mm firing sequence against a simulated target. You should mark this section with a tab or paperclip to be able to find it quickly for reference when needed from time to time.

Appendix B and *Appendix F* are aircrew lists for the gunships and ABCCC, respectively. This is the only place in the manuscript where names for all aircrews are listed by aircrew position.

In *Appendix C – AC-130H Firing with External Fuel Tanks*, I describe the live fire test flown in 1980 that determined it was non-destructive and safe to fire each of the guns with the external fuel tanks installed. Because of the findings in that test, this was the first mission where the gunship was deployed non-stop to a theater of operations using multiple air refuelings, and then employed having all guns available to fire immediately upon arrival in the combat area.

In *Appendix D – Air Refueling from the KC-10*, potential gunship problems associated with the air force's newest tanker are resolved with the modified procedures and additional training syllabus developed during a test mission as part of the KC-10's IOT&E. Consequently, several crews had their first time KC-10 air refueling without difficulty.

Appendix E – EC-130E Airborne Battlefield Command and Control Center (ABCCC) - I wanted to say a few more nice things about ABCCC before I was done, but couldn't fit them into the context of the piece that appears at the beginning of Chapter 3. This appendix talks briefly about the airframe and the crew positions. I closed with the system's obituary, but wanted all to know that a piece of that combat veteran's system (the capsule) survives here at Eglin's Air Armament Museum, and is waiting to see you anytime you're in the neighborhood.

ET CETERA

All of the mission time lines are based on Greenwich Mean Time (GMT), aka Zulu (Z). Mission times used in the narrative are local times unless otherwise noted. Both Grenada and Barbados local times are GMT minus four hours.

At the time of this writing, I am telling a story based on the AC-130H gunship weapon's equipment package that existed in 1983 on airframes built in 1969. At the time of Grenada the airplanes were already 14 years old and had not significantly changed since they flew in Vietnam in the 1970's. Our single new high-tech piece of equipment was the satellite communications (SATCOM) UHF radio that was installed for use during the Iran Hostage rescue mission in 1980. At that time the antenna was externally mounted on the top center escape hatch as a temporary fix, and it was still "temporarily" mounted for Grenada three years later. Although not updated with new equipment, the airplane was still very capable of doing the job and the crews were well trained to make that happen, there just weren't any high-tech bells and whistles that you might find on today's newer model gunships.

I have also frozen in time the policies and procedures described herein. Everything is vintage 1983, and in no way reflects on the current operating practices used today even for the same airframes.

SAFETY CONCERNS

The ground track of a gunship's nominal orbit is roughly two miles in diameter. Any two gunships working targets within one mile of each other will have overlapping orbits and must maintain vertical separation of at least 500 ft.

Standard gunship procedures at the time did not address (two aircraft) firing in overlapping or concentric orbits. In the situation of overlapping orbits over Grenada, where both aircraft must be ready to fire when required, non-standard safety procedures were established by the crews that required the higher altitude aircraft's safety scanners to have eyes-on the lower aircraft to insure clearance prior to firing. Plane-to-plane communications were established and maintained on company frequency.

If a third aircraft was stacked in the same orbit it was non-firing only, and would perform recce duties. Ground FACs usually did not give firing assignments to more than one aircraft at a time, but the non-firing second aircraft in the stack could be called upon (depending upon the urgency) to shoot should the lower firing aircraft have a fire control or weapon problem.

Navy aircraft and Army helicopters flew uncontrolled in the battle area, and did not always adjust their route of flight to remain clear of gunship live fire operations. Gunship crews had to exercise additional vigilance while firing to assure the safety of this wayward traffic.

ABOUT THE BATTLE AREA

Grenada lies at the southernmost tip of the Windward Islands in the southeastern Caribbean Sea. The capital is St. George's (notice the unusual "possessive" form). The airport's name at the time was Point Salines (pronounced sa-leenz, not sa-li-nas) Airport (PSA). It has since been designated an International airport.

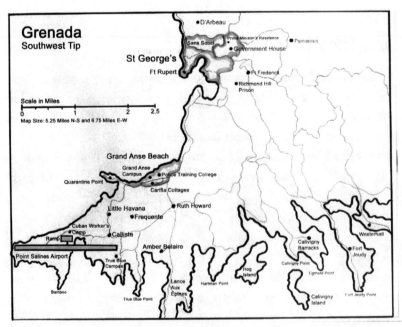

Figure 4. Map of the southwestern part of the battle area showing all the principal locations.

GRENADA GRINDER

The geographical size of the battle area in southwest Grenada was quite small, only 56 square miles, 7 miles east-west by 8 miles north-south. A gunship flying at orbit airspeed can move from any target within the area to any other target in four minutes or less. Figure 4 shows the southwest part of the battle area where all of the gunship live-fire and most of the armed reconnaissance occurred. The missing part to the north covers the area around Beausejour which is the site of the Radio Free Grenada station.

Also not shown on the battle area map is Pearls Airport, a 5000 ft non-lighted asphalt strip located on the northeast coast of the island. This airport lies in the area where the U.S. Navy and Marines came ashore to capture the northern part of the island. It plays a very limited part in the gunship story.

CHAPTER 1
PRE-MISSION

SQUADRON ALERT AND RECALL

In the early evening of Friday, 21 Oct 1983, the operations Duty Officer from my unit, the 16th Special Operations Squadron (SOS), called me at home and put me on telephone alert. Translated, that meant pack bags for possible deployment for 30 days, stay put at home near the phone (no cell phones back in the day), be ready to report for duty within 30 minutes of being called, and most importantly, be rested and ready to fly.

The first thing I did, of course, was to try to figure out what was going on because the caller didn't give a reason on the phone, and probably couldn't due to a security restriction. At that time my guess was that the only situation with the possible outbreak of hostility was Beirut. The United States Marines had been in a peacekeeping role there since March and the US Embassy in Beirut had been bombed in April. Beirut was on the TV news and in the newspapers every day. That had to be it.

I was convinced that I was right when on 23 Oct 1983, it was reported in all the media that the Marines' Headquarters building and barracks in Beirut had been destroyed by a terrorist, and 241 Americans had been killed. Surely that was it and the phone would ring any second now.

On 24 Oct 1983 at 1500 local, I finally got the telephone recall to report to the squadron, still not knowing the exact reason. As soon as I arrived everything seemed hectic and rushed as I went through my preflight sequence. I quickly checked the Pilot's Information File for updates and signed-in by initialing the Flight Orders. Our Air Traffic Control (ATC) call sign was Rider 10, tactical call sign Lima (lee-ma) 56, tail number 69-6575, with an augmented crew of 18 (extra pilot, navigator, flight engineer, and illuminator operator). As I checked my oxygen mask and tested the interphone in my flight helmet at the personal equipment counter, the Duty Officer hurried me along by announcing that all my crewmembers were already onboard the crew bus waiting for me. It was at the front door ready to take us to the Mobility hangar for temporary duty (TDY) processing.

Everything with the pre-mission process was abnormal that afternoon, including the fact that we had been shorted an hour of pre-mission time usually reserved for crew study and briefing preparation. Why were they rushing me? Something big must be getting ready to happen.

All crewmembers participating in a large scale TDY mission are required to process through the Mobility processing line. At consecutive stations in the line you accomplish some particular task that prepares you for the TDY. These would include: verify personal information and receive copies of TDY orders, review and verify personal emergency records, take issue of a .38-caliber Smith & Wesson revolver and ammunition, get a cash advance if you want it, and other similar reviews and actions. If all your records are current, it takes less than ten minutes and you're done.

From there the whole crew went directly to the large mission briefing room at the 8th Special Operations Squadron. Normally the enlisted crewmembers would have gone to the plane to perform their preflight inspections, but for this mission all crew pre-flights had already been completed.

MISSION BRIEFING

At the 8th SOS we were quickly ushered into the briefing room, greeted there by a lot of senior ranking officers from the Division and Wing Headquarters. No other crews were attending. As soon as we were seated near front center, the briefer's assistant passed out crew flimsies (i.e., mission folders) containing handouts for each crewmember on the fire control team. The mission briefer began by opening the curtain covering the flight planning maps and mission timing chart.

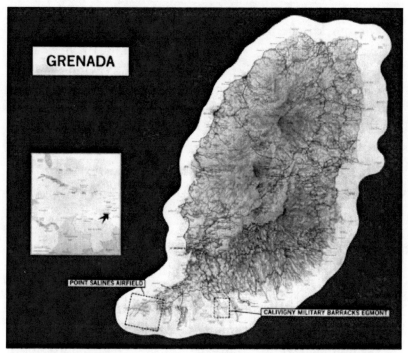

Figure 5. Grenada. Southernmost tip of the Windward Islands, 1350 nm
SE of Miami

Then he said, "Today's mission is to rescue United States citizens who are medical students on the island of **GRENADA!**" In my mind I drew a blank, "Where's Grenada?" He continued with the mission overview followed by operational details. A staff navigator then briefed mission times and air refueling details, followed by an intelligence briefing (discussed in detail in a following section), a weather briefing, and then we were done except for questions.

This briefing was an excellent example of the fire hose technique where more data is given to you in a very short period than you can easily assimilate. If we were lucky, all the briefed information should be somewhere in the handouts, and we would have plenty of time to study those while enroute.

The important point at this time was to ask questions for clarification about what wasn't clear or what you can't quickly find in the handouts, but we didn't have much time to do that. All too quickly the briefing was over and we were hurried out the door to our aircraft. As Pilot in Command, I reviewed and signed the completed Military Flight Plan (DD Form 175) that was in the flimsy, and on my way out handed it in for passing to the flight dispatcher at Base Operations.

Well it turned out that I was totally wrong with my assumptions and my guesses. The alert on 21 Oct 1983 had nothing to do with Beirut. That date, as we now know but a closely guarded secret at the time, was the date that the National Security Council issued National Security Decision Directive (NSDD) 110, signed by President Reagan, which was guidance to the Secretary of Defense and the Joint Chiefs of Staff (JCS) to begin contingency planning for a mission with an objective of:

"U.S. participation in a multi-lateral effort to restore order on Grenada and deter Cuban military intervention." [1]

The tasking obviously translated into a need for combat forces and the alert was part of the implementation of that tasking down to our wing organization level.

On 23 Oct 1983, the National Security Council issued NSDD 110A in which President Reagan directed the operation to begin before dawn on 25 Oct 1983 with the a three-fold objective of:

"(1) Assuring the safety of American citizens on Grenada, (2) In conjunction with other Organization of Eastern Caribbean States (OECS) friendly government participants, the restoration of democratic government on Grenada, and(3) The elimination of current, and the prevention of further, Cuban intervention in Grenada." [2]

UNPLANNED CONTINGENCIES

As I walked out of the briefing I had no clue that several component plans of the mission were already going wrong and would cause problems later on. A lot of activities were compartmentalized and thus were not evident to other joint players. Descriptions of these activities were not briefed or provided in handouts. Many problems were caused by the commanders at the higher command levels being incapable of adequately planning and being unable to bring in the appropriate staff planners due to the security restrictions. A brief list follows:

1. Army Special Forces' helicopters supported three missions: (1) the combined Army Ranger, Army Delta Force, and SEAL assault on Richmond Hill Prison (RHP); (2) the SEAL's capture of the Radio Free Grenada (RFG) station; and (3) the SEAL's rescue of Queen Elizabeth's representative on Grenada, Governor General Sir Paul Scoon.[1] Gunships were not briefed-in or given the opportunity to participate in any of the three. In fact we had no prior knowledge whatsoever of these missions.

The *2nd Air Division After Action Report* specifically discusses this lapse in planning and execution, and correctly states that at least one AC-130 was available to cover the assault on RHP at that time. Since the mission was executing behind schedule, three gunships were working overhead Point Salines Airport (PSA) at 0615 local time. If just one had been diverted to RHP it could possibly have prevented the loss of a UH-60 helicopter, its pilot, and several Special Forces members on the assault team.[2]

Both the RFG mission and the Scoon rescue mission should have had some kind of gunship support, either on stand-by or on-call, but at the very least have been mission briefed to the gunships so we would be aware of them just in case. The RFG mission, for example, could have ended in disaster with the SEALs making a water exit when they were overrun by PRA troops at the station. They floated offshore for several hours out of contact before a chance pickup by one of their ships.

The Scoon rescue mission would later drag out into a full 24-hour period and turn into the top priority mission for all U.S. forces.[3] It would be worked by each of the six gunships as a major on-call task at some point during their missions over that 24 hour period.

2. An Air Tasking Order (ATO) containing the Communications and Electronic Operating Instruction (CEOI) listing call signs and frequencies for all joint players had not been published by CINCLANT. This was probably the single most inexcusable and far reaching planning failure. As a result, cross-service communications were virtually impossible. For example, Navy A-7s couldn't talk with the Army Rangers or 82nd Airborne units, and AC-130 gunships couldn't talk with the SEALs, or A-7s, or Navy helicopters.

3. The Defense Mapping Agency was not notified well in advance of the Grenada mission by high-level planners.[4] Consequently, standard map coverage was not available until after the operation had already begun on 25 Oct 1983.[5] The only maps available for aircrew (and all joint forces) on Day-1 were inadequate black and white copies of a Grenadian "tourist" map that did not have standard military map features such as grid lines, marked hazards, colored elevations, etc. (Our "tourist" maps were issued to us in the crew flimsy during the crew briefing.)

4. It is evident that the objectives of NCA and JCS requests for target area photographs was not to support the warfighter. Aerial (and satellite) photographs of the Point Salines Airport area, the city of St. George's and environs, and Calivigny Barracks area, were not made available to the gunships.[6] Consequently, targets within these areas could not be positively identified unless clearly depicted on the maps or described by a ground Forward Air Controller (FAC). Photo-imagery of Grenada was requested by the National Command Authorities through the JCS on 21 Oct 83, and by the Defense Intelligence Agency on 22 Oct 83. SAC SR-71's flew the requested missions over Grenada on 22 and 23 Oct 83, respectively, to "furnish imagery that might help assess the Cuban/Soviet disposition."[7]

On 22 Oct 83, the JCS directed SAC to fly daily U-2R missions beginning on 23 Oct.[8] Unfortunately, after 22 Oct with almost continual cloud cover, the SAC recon efforts "provided meager information on the location of Grenadian military equipment." Listed locations photographed included Ft. Rupert, Pt. Salines Airport, Pearls Airport, Frequente Military Camp, and Ft. Frederick. [9] (Descriptions of specific equipment found at each location was redacted in the text of the referenced document.) All of these areas except the Pearls Airport were of specific interest to the gunships.

Although this marginal imagery may not have provided the specific information that Intelligence sources were looking for, it would have been invaluable in providing gunship crews with visual references to be able to positively identify possible targets and the local environs at those locations. (None of the aerial photographs of Grenada in this book were available to gunship aircrews on Day-1.)

5.   This war was planned to last one 24-hour period. [10] Contingency plans for follow-on efforts had not been developed. Immediate resupply of gunship ammunition was not available at any location in the theater on 25 Oct 1983. Adequate operating stocks of ammunition and full maintenance support from Hurlburt Field didn't arrive at Barbados via C-141 until 26 Oct 1983. [11]

6. Rules of Engagement (ROE) were not addressed in our briefing. [11] Fortunately, gunships already had standing ROEs that covered those imposed by this operation: minimize damage to non-military targets, avoid civilian casualties, avoid collateral damage, and do not to fire on a target unless directed and cleared by an appropriate agency (e.g., ground or air forward air controller). This final rule also bans pre-emptive firing. Gunships are always authorized defensive self-protection, however, against targets that demonstrate hostile intent.

7. Gunships were directed to recover at Roosevelt Roads, Puerto Rico, without exception. No alternate landing site was briefed. The airport at Barbados was not mentioned at all, neither for the possible use as an emergency recovery base nor as an

intermediate refueling stop. The significance of this point is that there is more that one hour difference in the flying time from Grenada to Roosevelt Roads versus from Grenada to Barbados. This would have made a significant difference, especially for Day-1, in that it would have permitted an additional hour on target over Grenada before reaching Bingo fuel (i.e., all the fuel remaining onboard is necessary for recovery plus required reserves). The availability of a tanker drives the decision at Bingo to either air refuel or RTB. The reason for the limitation on use of Barbados is explained in the following section.

COMMANDER OF AIRLIFT FORCES (COMALF) AND THE BARBADOS FORWARD OPERATING BASE

The compressed planning time for Operation Urgent Fury and the failure by high-level planners to bring in the day-to-day airlift experts in a timely manner caused considerable operational and logistics problems up front, specifically for the required follow-on effort. No plans existed for anything past "red light," the term used to signify the end of the airdrop/airland operational event. The non-use of Barbados at the time of our briefing was only fully explained with the recent declassification of the following document:

In an interview with the MAC History Office on 12 Sep 1984, Major General (then Brigadier General) Robert B. Patterson, 21st AF Commander, recounted the sequence of events regarding his appointment as Commander of Airlift Forces (COMALF) for Urgent Fury on 23 Oct 83, only two days before the start of the operation. He revealed how dire the situation was regarding the non-existence of plans for necessary intra-theater tactical airlift, follow-on strategic airlift support, forward operating base beddown locations, logistics support, etc., when he reported that same evening to CINCLANT Headquarters at Norfolk, VA, to begin work. [12]

Among other major problems, he was told initially on 24 Oct 83 that he **could not** use Grantley Adams International Airport, Barbados, only 145 nautical miles from Point Salines Airport, Grenada, as a Forward Operating Base (FOB). This restriction would force the use of Roosevelt Roads NAS, Puerto Rico, over 430 nautical miles from Grenada, as the FOB. Later that day he was told that he **could** use Barbados, but too late for notification of the change to make its way down through the system. He could not for operational security reasons call the airport management before his arrival and ask about aircraft parking, ground support, workspace facilities, or most importantly, the availability of jet fuel. None of this information for the entire operation was available pre-mission except for the airfield data described in the Flight Planning documents used by aircrews. [13]

Fortunately, with a small staff of highly qualified and experienced experts that had worked with him on several exercises, he was able to quickly overcome most of the logistical and support problems upon his arrival at Barbados on the 25th at 0246L on the C-5(s) that brought in the Army's Special Operations helicopters. Arrangements for jet fuel, ground transportation, crew and support personnel billeting, operations and maintenance workspace, and many other similar requirements were quickly contracted. [12]

Undoubtedly the key to the whole operation was the availability of aircraft fuel. Luckily, the Texaco/Shell airport fuel contractors reported that they had a "million pounds" of JP-4 jet fuel (and could get more if needed) and the necessary fuel trucks to quickly service the aircraft for quick turnarounds. Shortly after announcing on the SATCOM Command Net that refueling was available at Barbados, the refueling capability was thoroughly tested early on the 25th when numerous Special Operations C-130's in the stream of aircraft delivering the Army Special Forces to Grenada stopped for fuel before returning to the CONUS. The requirement for fuel for Special Operations aircraft and transient MAC aircraft continued throughout the operation until the close of hostilities in November 1983. [13]

Although the Spectre gunships were not "airlift" per se, we were indeed MAC assets through our parent command of 23rd Air Force and 2nd Air Division. As such we were fully supported (i.e., billeting, transportation, ammunition, parts, etc.) by the COMALF and the airlift FOB team through the 21st AF Logistics channels.[14] Although the ABCCC aircraft and crews were a TAC asset they were nonetheless fully supported in the same way. Both units had their own maintenance teams.

THE INTELLIGENCE BRIEFING

The Intelligence (Intel) portion of the crew briefing provided very little definitive information about the current anti-aircraft artillery (AAA) threat at the Point Salines Airport. It contained the latest Defense Intelligence Agency (DIA) estimates from the 16 Oct 1983 satellite pictures that were passed to Joint Special Operations Command (JSOC) J2 (Intelligence), but contained more background than hard, usable current Intel.[1] The briefing points were as follows:

1. At no time during analysis or ground reports was any type of AAA noted at Point Salines Airfield.

2. Aircrews were advised that the 2-barrel 23mm ZU-23 and the 4-barrel 14.5 mm ZPU-4 AAA weapons were in the Grenadian inventory, but the latest Intel showed these weapons to be in garrison and not deployed to the field.[2]

3. Aircrews were also briefed that a lot of (military) truck movements at night were noted going toward Point Salines airfield, but Defense Intelligence Agency (DIA) assumed it was in support of the construction activity.

Much to the credit of Lt Paul Darby and TSgt Don Corbin, the Special Operations intelligence team at Hurlburt Field, the position held by other Intel analysts that the weapons remained in garrison was rejected. Although no hard Intel was available to prove it, just other contributing facts and conclusions, their interpretation of these points was that the presence of air defense weapons at the airport could not be ruled out. Based on their interpretation, they added a cautious "better safe than sorry" warning to our briefing as the most prudent course of action.[3]

After the briefing the gunship operations briefer, Maj Al Collette, came up to Capt Locklear and me to express his concerns about the AAA situation as briefed by Intel. His concern strengthened our position that we should wisely expect the airfield to be well defended.

THE ACTUAL THREAT

The Grenadian AAA defenses actually facing the gunship (See Table 1) were comprised of older Soviet-bloc 12.7mm and 23mm guns, both still formidable, lethal threats to slow, low-flying aircraft. Post-war listings of quantities for each type of gun were found in either captured documents or surrendered weapon inventories and are presented here.

For the quad 12.7mm gun, a captured 1981 Grenadian memo shows that 12 each were received from Cuba in 1979 along with 237,000 rounds of ammunition.[4] A single 12.7mm gun in the quad is roughly the equivalent of the U.S. 50-caliber gun.

For the 23mm guns, a Dec 1983 Department of Defense brochure of captured weapons showed that 12 each were available for use against U.S. forces with over 86,000 rounds still remaining at the end of the day on 25 Oct 1983.[5] The 23mm gun can shoot either an armor-piercing incendiary tracer round (API-T) or a high-explosive incendiary tracer round (HEI-T). An HEI-T round, for example, can reach an airplane flying at 6000 ft above ground level in approximately 2-3 seconds and explosively detonate on impact. It airbursts at over 11,000 ft if it misses.[6]

Rounds from both guns are lethal. Rounds that may hit the gunship (or any aircraft) will certainly cause damage, depending on the type and size of the bullet and where it hits. Severity could range from simple 12.7mm entrance and exit bullet holes through the skin without hitting anything, to a 23mm round that detonates under the aircraft skin causing damage to any number of functional parts, especially fuel, electric, hydraulic, etc. The 23mm round particularly has the energy to penetrate, detonate, and cause considerable localized internal damage, and has the incendiary feature to start a fire if it hits any ignitable object. A round from either gun into the cockpit area has a special lethality for obvious reasons.

Table 1. Anti-Aircraft Artillery (AAA) on Grenada

Crew Served Weapons[1] *(Altitude in Feet, Rate of Fire in rounds per minute per barrel)*

Type	No.	Description	Eff Alt	Max Alt	Rate of Fire	Cyclic Rate of Fire
DShKM-4	12	Quad-barrel 12.7mm AA gun	3000	16800	80 rpm/b	540-600 rpm/b
ZU-23	12	Twin-barrel 23mm AA gun	6036	15300	200 rpm/b	800-1000 rpm/b

Round Types and Characteristics

Caliber	Type	Weight	Muzzle Velocity	Airburst
12.7mm	API	1.75 oz	2520 ft/sec	-
23mm	API-T	0.42 lb	2910 ft/sec	-
23mm	HEI-T	0.42 lb	2910 ft/sec	11340 ft

Reported Locations[2]

Type	No.	Location	Organization
DShKM-4	2	Point Salines AP	Cuban Defenses
DShKM-4	1	Grand Anse	PRA Rapid Mobilization
DShKM-4	1	Ruth Howard	PRA Rapid Mobilization
DShKM-4	2	Pearls Airport	
DShKM-4	2	Fort Frederick	RMC Headquarters
DShKM-4	2	Fort Rupert	PRA Headquarters
DShKM-4	2	D'Arbeau Hill	PRA - North of City of St. George's
ZU-23	2	Point Salines AP	Cuban Defenses
ZU-23	2	Point Salines AP	Cuban Defenses
ZU-23	2	Frequente	PRA - Logistics Headquarters
ZU-23	2	Fort Frederick	RMC Headquarters
ZU-23	2	Fort Rupert	PRA Headquarters
ZU-23	2	Mt. Parnassus	PRA Battle Group - 2 km northeast of St. George's

Deployed locations shown in Table 1 are generally based on the reference, then adjusted to be consistent with what the gunships encountered.[7] Both the 12.7mm and the 23mm guns are towable, and some were assigned to mobile defense units, so they could have been encountered anywhere. It should be noted that several guns of both types may have been un-manned due to shortages of trained crews and the failure of the People's Revolutionary Militia crews to show up for duty when the alert was sounded.[8]

(Top) Figure 6. DShKM-4 12.7mm AAA gun
(Bottom) Figure 7. ZU-23 23mm 2-barrel AAA gun
captured at Ft Rupert. The 4-barrel version is the ZSU-23.

INVASION TONIGHT

The underlying assumption in the three main points of the Intelligence briefing was that the air defense weapons were in a benign state and not positioned for an effective air defense. One could also safely assume that if Grenadian forces were alerted with some threatening activity, like an invasion, that readiness of those defenses would necessarily change.

That's exactly what happened. On 22 Oct 1983, as reported worldwide in the Associated Press (AP) wire service and on the evening news courtesy of CBS, the USS Independence Carrier Group, already at sea headed for Lebanon, changed course for Grenada.[9]

Each day for the next several days AP reported new developments and the reactions of the Grenadian government and the surrounding Caribbean states (paraphrased in Table 2). By the evening of the 24th, Radio Free Grenada was reporting "invasion tonight." It is also apparent that they assumed that Point Salines Airport would be attacked since they armed it to the teeth. The only thing they didn't know was the exact time, and ironically, the joint forces didn't know that either because it kept changing.

All of this news was reported on the International wire service and in the newspapers, albeit for us hidden in the back pages of our local newspaper. I may have seen the articles but I surely didn't connect the dots. At the time of the briefing we thought that operational security had been maintained and the invasion was close-hold and still a classified operation.

It is a fact that Hurlburt's Intel knew that the mission's cover had been blown. Information from one of the newspaper articles had provided support for their conclusion regarding the probable presence of air defense weapons at the Point Salines Airport.[10] It would seem to me that they would want me (and the other crews) to have that piece of information for planning our tactics. So why weren't we briefed on this development? We shouldn't have to whisper and tiptoe around if nobody's sleeping.

Table 2 - They Knew We Were Coming

Articles from the *Playground Daily News*, Ft Walton Beach, FL, with publication date as indicated:

Associated Press, Washington DC, "U.S. Marines heading for Grenada", 22 Oct 1983 [1]

- Some 2000 Marines and the aircraft carrier USS Independence headed for troubled island

- Moves designed to protect lives of estimated 1000 Americans if evacuation needed

- Marines were in a group with amphibious assault ship USS Guam headed for Lebanon

- The carrier and Marine group will remain out of sight of land unless needed for evacuation

- Possibility exists that only airport would be closed and Americans could not evacuate

Associated Press, Port-of-Spain, Trinidad, "Grenada accuses U.S. of concocting invasion excuse", 23 Oct 1983 [2]

- Grenada's leftist military junta says U.S. invented reports that American residents are in danger

- State-run Radio Free Grenada reports that Gen Hudson Austin says U.S. claims are pretext for invasion

- Grenada believed to have about 800 soldiers, but size of militia is unclear

- Radio monitored on Barbados where Caribbean Prime Ministers are meeting to consider sanctions

- Access to island difficult because government has banned journalists and closed the airport

Associated Press, Port-of-Spain, Trinidad, "Caribbean leaders rap Grenada; radio warns of 'invasion'", 24 Oct 1983 [3]

- Eastern Caribbean leaders called Grenada's new military government a threat to regional security

- Radio Free Grenada broadcast said "an invasion of our country is expected tonight"
- Witness reports that 120-150 soldiers from other Caribbean nations arrived at Barbados airport
- Four U.S. diplomats returned from Grenada on Sunday after visiting Americans

Associated Press, Bridgetown, Barbados, "U.S. Marines spotted on Caribbean Island; Grenada mission eyed", 25 Oct 1983 [4]

- About 50 Marines landed here Monday and immediately flew out on three helicopters
- Associated Press reported seeing Marines in combat gear board two Sea King helicopters with Huey gunship
- U.S. Embassy spokesman says, "What you are seeing could be used as part one of the options to effect a departure of the Americans (from Grenada) and to ensure their security."

REPORTS OF ADVANCED STATE DEPARTMENT NOTICE

From time to time during my research I kept running across un-substantiated reports of a pre-invasion communication from the U.S. State Department to Havana advising them of the impending invasion. The implication was that in their zeal to satisfy the requirement in National Security Decision Directive 110A to "... inform Cuba and the Soviet Union of our actions at an appropriate time ...", the State Department jumped the gun and advised them before the event took place, thereby jeopardizing the whole operation and the lives of participating U.S. servicemen. [1]

I finally found a good reference for such a report in the November 14, 1983, issue of TIME magazine, *Now to Make it Work*, page 23, "Even the U.S. State Department told Havana just hours before the invasion that the strike was imminent, assuring Castro that it was not aimed at his workers. This tip-off angered the Pentagon." [2]

I also found that in fact the Washington Times ran an article a few days earlier in its November 9, 1983, edition that made a similar assertion. At that time a State Department spokesman told the newspaper in reply that these and similar reports were totally false, but the Times had only reported the denials without comment. [3]

The subject re-surfaced again, however, in a Washington Times newspaper article on January 2, 1984, with more discussions in additional articles on January 5 and 6, 1984. This time the State Department took issue. [4]

This time using a more public approach, the State Department wrote a "Letter to the Editor" of the Washington Times dated January 9, 1984. In the letter, Under Secretary of State for Political Affairs, Lawrence S. Eagleburger, permanently put the issue to rest more directly. He said, "This call occurred approximately three hours after the operation had commenced and our troops were on the ground." He later adds, "We had no intention of giving the Cubans advanced notice of the rescue mission on Grenada and did not do so." [5]

The State Department's original intent was to notify the government of Cuba at an early hour when they had already received field reports of the invasion but still had time to order their forces not to resist, thereby saving both American and Cuban lives. The communications link State had planned to use had been cut by the Cubans the previous day and had not yet been repaired causing the time delay of the actual notification. [6]

NOTES - CHAPTER 1

MISSION BRIEFING
1. The White House, *National Security Decision Directive 110*, 1.
2. The White House, *National Security Decision Directive 110A*, 1.

UNPLANNED CONTINGENCIES
1. *2nd Air Division After Action Report*, 57.
2. Ibid.
3. Kulielski, *Grenada: Five Years Later*, A-12.

4. Cole, *Operation Urgent Fury*, 20.
5. Carney, *No Room for Error*, 297.
6. *2nd Air Division After Action Report*, 59.
7. *Urgent Fury: The United States Air Force and the Grenada Operation*, 24.
8. Ibid., 25.
9. Ibid., 26 & 27.
10. *History of 2nd Air Division*, 127.
11. Colonel Robertson interview, 17 Apr 2007.
12. *History of 2nd Air Division*, 164.
14. Kallander, MGen Patterson interview, 12 Sep 1984, 1.
15. Ibid., 3.
16. Ibid., 9.
17. Ibid., 8.
18. Ibid., 13.

THE INTELLIGENCE BRIEFING
1. *2nd Air Division After Action Report*, 54. *History of 2nd Air Division*, 156.
2. The quad-barreled anti-aircraft gun in the Grenadian inventory was briefed by Intel to be the 14.5mm ZPU-4. Post mission photos of captured weapons showed it to actually be the quad- barreled Czechoslovakian 12.7mm M53 Anti-aircraft Machine Gun using the Soviet DShKM-4. The M53 has a lower rate of fire than the ZPU-4, and also has a smaller effective lethal envelope. 3. *History of 2nd Air Division*, 157.
4. Dept of State & Dept of Defense, *Grenada: A Preliminary Report*, 22.
5. Dept of Defense, *Grenada: October 25 to November 2, 1983*, 3-1.
6. Cullen, *Jane's Land-Based Air Defence 1990-91*, 226.
7. Adkin, *Urgent Fury*, 163.
8. Ibid., 165.
9. Cole, *Operation Urgent Fury*, 20.
10. *History of 2nd Air Division*, 157.

TABLE 1. ANTI-AIRCRAFT ARTILLERY (AAA) ON GRENADA
1. Cullen, *Jane's Land-Based Air Defence 1990-91*, 177-178 & 226-228. Note the 2-barrel 23mm is designated the "ZU", the quad-barrel 23mm is the "ZSU".
2. Adkin, *Urgent Fury*, 163.

TABLE 2. THEY KNEW WE WERE COMING
1. Playground Daily News, *U.S. Marines heading for Grenada.*

2. Playground Daily News, *Grenada Accuses U.S. of concocting invasion excuse*, 8A.
3. Playground Daily News, *Caribbean leaders rap Grenada*, 3B.
4. Playground Daily News, *U.S. Marines spotted on Caribbean island.*

REPORT OF ADVANCED STATE DEPARTMENT NOTICE
1. The White House, *National Security Decision Directive 110A*, 2.
2. TIME, *Now to Make It Work*, 23. 3. Eagleburger, *Letters to the Editor*, 1.
4. Ibid.
5. Ibid.
6. Ibid., 2.

CHAPTER 2
DAY ONE

AT THE AIRCRAFT

Our aircraft was parked in the run-up area at the north end of the Hurlburt Field runway. When we arrived, a host of extra people, all trying to help, greeted us in addition to the normal maintenance personnel. All aircraft inspections were complete, ammunition already loaded, and the plane was ready to go. I reviewed the maintenance status in the aircraft forms (AFTO 781) with the Flight Engineers, and was hurried along by the Maintenance Officer. He was very perturbed when I started on my usual 5-minute walk-around inspection to make sure everything was buttoned-up and ready to go. He just wanted to be sure that we made good our scheduled takeoff time of 1730 local time. I knew we could make up a few minutes if we needed to since we were already parked adjacent to the active runway and didn't have far to taxi.

With both Illuminator Operators (IO) standing by [1], I reviewed and signed the Weight and Balance Form F (DD Form 365 F) that showed we weighed exactly the authorized Emergency War Plan (EWP) allowable of 175,000 lbs, fully 20,000 lbs more than our normal everyday maximum gross weight.[2] The extra weight was in fuel in the external tanks and extra cans of ammunition strapped down in the aisle abeam the sensor booth.

I was confident that our two IOs, TSgt Gary Carter and SSgt Roy Duncan, had checked and re-checked every detail, and the numbers on the Form F were correct, particularly that the location of the center of gravity (CG) was within allowable limits. If the CG is out of limits, that means the airplane is either nose-heavy or tail-heavy, and won't fly right. Trying to fly an AC-130 weighing 175,000 lbs with either one of these conditions is against regulations, contrary to proper procedures, extremely dangerous, and most of all, just plain dumb.

They also said that we had extra flight lunches for everybody to provide a couple of meals each plus snacks, and an extra couple of large thermos of coffee. It could be a long time before we would be done for the day, so having enough food on board was extremely important.

The AC-130H ammunition Combat Load that can be stored in the built-in racks is shown in Table 3 below. The extra 20mm and 40mm ammunition loaded on our aircraft is shown in the right column:

Table 3. Lima 56 Ammunition Load

Gun #	Caliber	Combat Load	Extra Ammunition for Urgent Fury[1]
1	20 mm	1500 rounds	500 rounds (Stored in shipping cans)
2	20 mm	1500 rounds	500 rounds (Stored in shipping cans)
3	7.62 mm	0	Gun not installed. Too small for ops.
4	7.62 mm	0	Gun not installed. Too small for ops.
5	40 mm	256 rounds*	160 rounds (Stored in shipping cans)*
6	105 mm	100 rounds	0-No extra storage racks available

* Most of the 40mm rounds loaded on all the Urgent Fury aircraft were HEI-P Misch metal incendiary rounds. Upon impact with the target, Misch explodes into white hot fragments and sets fire to any part of the target that will burn. Any reference to a burning target after the 40mm was fired was due to being hit by 40mm Misch.

Before I went forward to get into the left pilot's seat to start engines, I called everybody together for a quick crew briefing. We numbered 18 with the extra pilot, flight engineer, navigator, and illuminator operator instead of the usual 14 on a normal mission (See Appendix B). I covered the required checklist items and then talked specifically about the mission and the probable profile. This would be the first combat mission for most of the young guys and it was important to me that they understood what to expect. After all questions were answered and everybody seemed happy with the information, I called for station time in five minutes time. At that time the crewmembers must be at their respective crew stations, be on headset for check-in on the interphone, and ready to begin the Before Starting Engines checklist.

TAKEOFF FROM HURLBURT

After starting engines and checking them with a thorough run-up, we completed all the checklist items and were ready to go. The copilot, Maj Scott Stephens, called for takeoff clearance:

"Hurlburt Tower, Rider One-zero, ready for takeoff." [1]

"Rider One-Zero, Hurlburt Tower. Wind 360 at 5 (knots), cleared for takeoff runway 18."

"Contact departure control when airborne."

"Rider One-zero, roger. Cleared for takeoff."

I set the throttles at maximum power, let the engines stabilize, and then released the brakes on the hack at 2230 Greenwich Mean Time (Z) (1730 local, CDST). The bird felt very heavy as we rolled down the 9600 ft runway, increasing speed ever so slowly. At the prescribed five knots below computed takeoff speed, I raised the nose to the normal nose-up takeoff attitude, but she didn't immediately fly off the runway as it normally would. We rolled and rolled, and finally as the end of the runway was coming up, I pulled on the yoke harder to raise the nose higher and she finally flew off well above the computed takeoff speed and near the end of the runway. After we were clear of the runway and safely airborne, I called for landing gear up, and then directed the copilot to milk (i.e., slowly raise) the flaps up as we slowly gained airspeed to our climb speed of 180 knots.

The longer takeoff roll was the first indication of degraded performance due to being heavier than our normal mission gross weight. Not really a big problem now that we were safely airborne, but I could expect a much slower than usual climb to our cruise altitude of 9000 ft. The effects of the heavier gross weight would become a more significant problem later on after we rendezvoused with the KC-135 tanker aircraft for our two enroute air refuelings.

Due to the tight air refueling schedule and the importance of reconnoitering the Point Salines Airport runway as early as possible, I elected to save time by skipping the sensor alignment and wet boresight (aka "tweak") procedures normally performed overhead Hurlburt Field and on the Eglin Range. Lt Col Paul Wonderly, our Fire Control Officer, had flown this airplane within the last few days and confirmed from his personal records that it was a good "shooter." In actuality we would later accomplish both procedures during the recce and initial live fire segments of the mission.

As we continued to climb, we turned easterly as directed by Eglin Departure Control, then after a handoff to Jacksonville Center, we intercepted the low altitude airway to Jacksonville, FL, then out over water via our flight planned route.

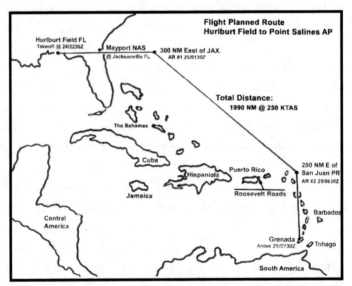

Figure 8.   Flight planned route from Hurlburt Field to Point Salines Airport, Grenada

The flight planned route was to proceed to a point 300 nautical miles (nm) east of Jacksonville where we would rendezvous and air refuel (AR) from our first tanker at 0130Z, then turn southeast and proceed to a point 250 nm east of San Juan, Puerto Rico (to remain clear of the San Juan Flight Information Region (FIR)), where we would rendezvous and AR from our second tanker at 0530Z. Missed air refueling alternate airports for the first and second AR were Jacksonville NAS (Mayport), FL, and Roosevelt Roads NAS, Puerto Rico, respectively.

The flight planned distance was 1990 nautical miles with an estimated time enroute of 7 1/2 hours at 250 knots true airspeed, plus an extra 30 minutes for a slower airspeed during the two air refuelings, estimated total time of eight hours to overhead the Point Salines Airport, Grenada.

A route of flight that would remain outside of the eastern boundary of the San Juan Flight Information Region (FIR) was a requirement placed on the gunship planners by civilian "suits" (i.e., FBI) representing certain federal government agencies. They were adamant that this restriction be observed. The expressed concern was that information regarding the presence of a stream of aircraft heading in the direction of Grenada might find its way from suspect FIR flight controllers to an unfriendly neighboring government (i.e., Cuba) at a most inopportune time.[2]

MISSION TIME LINE

The Mission Time Line for Lima 56 (Couvillon) is shown in Table 4. All times are GMT. Subtract four (4) hours from GMT to calculate the Grenada local time used in the narrative. For all intents and purposes, all times are listed exactly as recorded from debriefs, or were easily calculated from previous or succeeding events. Some obvious time and event errors were found and corrected.

The information is presented in tabular form to enable the reader to easily track the crew's mission events at any given time point. Moreover, it facilitates the comparison with the other mission aircraft time lines that are shown later in Chapter 5, Table 5 through Table 9.

The Event column briefly describes the mission's activities. The intention is to show the more significant activities for which a time and a description are available in the references.

It is highly probable that other less significant events were completed and not reported.

Table 4. Lima 56 (Couvillon) Mission Time Line

Time (Z)	Event
24/2230	Takeoff Hurlburt Field, FL, at gross weight of 175,000 lbs
25/0130	Air refuel #1 (night) with KC-135 to 170,000 lbs
0630	Air refuel #2 (night) with KC-135 to 175,000 lbs
0730	Arrived overhead Point Salines Airport (PSA) at 9,000 ft to recce runway
0745	Departed PSA for out-of-sight hold point several miles south of the island
0815	UHF SATCOM radio totally fails. Unable to communicate on command net
0850	Arrived orbit overhead Ft Jeudy at 6000 ft
0915	Made first radio contact with Lima 58 (Twiford)
0945	Departed Ft Jeudy orbit. Destroyed 23mm AAA target near Frequente
0950	Arrived PSA orbit at 6000 ft. Worked Ranger TIC at PSA and vicinity
1130	Bingo fuel. Departed PSA for air refuel #3 with KC-10 to 173,000#
1215	Returned to orbit PSA. On-call for Ranger TIC support. Put on stand-by
1230	Departed to re-tweak #6 gun (105mm) overwater south of PSA
1330	Worked Little Havana Cuban HQ compound target with Lima 57 (Sims)
1345	Destroyed Ft Rupert target on peninsula in city of St. George's
1415	Tasked to support SEALs protecting Sir Paul Scoon at Government House
1430	Lima 57 (Sims) joins to support SEALs overhead Government House
1500	Bingo fuel. Depart Grenada for Roosevelt Roads, Puerto Rico
1700	Landed Roosevelt Roads. Refueled. Directed to proceed to Barbados
1836	Takeoff Roosevelt Roads for Barbados
2040	Landed Grantley Adams Airport, Barbados. RON. Day-1 complete
2230	Face-to-face operational crew brief to Strelau's crew
26/1702	Takeoff Barbados for Day-2 mission to Grenada
1740	Tasked to recce Quarantine Point. Observed APC but no firing clearance
1755	Arrive orbit overhead PSA. On-call for Ranger TIC support
1915	Attacked 40 Carifta Cottages target across street from Grand Anse campus
1925	Attacked police training college target north of Grand Anse campus. Burned
1945	Attacked bunkered 12.7mm AAA site target ½ km NE of training college
2000	Armed recce to support rescue of medical students from Grand Anse campus
2330	Depart orbit PSA
27/0011	Landed Barbados. Day-2 mission complete
0401	Depart Barbados to reposition to Roosevelt Roads for continued ops
0725	Arrive Roosevelt Roads
30 Oct-2 Nov	Three Armed Recce missions of four hours on-station
30-Oct	Supported 82nd Abn troops for capture of RMC leader, Gen Hudson Austin
03/1148	Depart Roosevelt Roads for return to Hurlburt Field, FL
03/1730	Arrive Hurlburt Field. Mission complete

References for times in the Tables as well as in the narratives are contained in the following documents:

1. History of the 2nd Air Division, 129 – 146
2. 2nd Air Division After Action Report, 16 – 25
3. Colonel Cox's Urgent Fury Trip Book, 99 – 104

GRENADA GRINDER

On or about 27th or the 28th of October 1983, the gunships began flying Armed Recce missions without any further live fire support, in gunship parlance a "dry fire." These continued until the aircraft were released and redeployed to Hurlburt Field. For each crew's Time Line, these flights have been summarized to show mission count with only existing major event detail.

ENROUTE AIR REFUEL

The first air refuel (AR) of two while enroute was scheduled for 0130Z at a point 300 nautical miles (nm) east of Jacksonville, FL. We made both the Air Refueling Control Point (ARCP) and the Air Refueling Control Time (ARCT) good, and the KC-135 tanker executed a point parallel rendezvous right on the money and rolled out about one nm in front of us. I was flying in the pilot's (left) seat and Maj Scott Stephens was in the copilot's (right) seat. Both this first AR and the second were at night which always makes things more exciting.

Figure 9. AC-130H on the boom taking fuel from a KC-135 tanker

Typically in a normal AR rendezvous in a non-combat situation, the tanker and the receiver make standard radio calls to each other to denote progress. For this mission, both air refueling tracks were in close proximity to either Cuba or the target area, particularly for the second AR. In this sensitive situation of not wanting to alert any "bad guys" who might be listening, the plan was to use the "radio silent" procedure where everything is assumed to be OK and normal radio calls are not made.

If needed to report a problem or to make a request, a set of standardized cockpit-to-boomer (the boom operator is aka "the boomer") light signals are used where the number of flashes or movement of the light has a coded meaning. When in contact with the boom and taking fuel, however, most tankers had the Through the Boom (TTB) intercom system that allowed direct receiver pilot-to-boomer verbal communications. Of course in an emergency or safety situation, a brief radio call could always be made.

All went well through pre-contact and contact positions, and then the problem started. Normally at contact when the refueling boom is inserted into the receiver's receptacle, latches in the receptacle grip the boom and hold it in-place. For some unknown reason, ours were not engaging, bad news to be sure. I disconnected, had the flight engineer reset the system and moved back into contact again. Same problem again, still no latches.

There is a refueling option, however, that is possible without the boom latches in place using a method called "stiff boom" where the tanker's boom operator maintains extension pressure to keep the boom in place.[1] At the time (in 1983), stiff boom was classified as an operational emergency procedure, only to be used in dire circumstances. I decided our situation certainly qualified after thinking about it for maybe 5 milliseconds, I told the KC-135 boomer to "STIFF BOOM" through the TTB that was still working during our brief contact, and he acknowledged.

Again I moved up into the contact position, the boomer inserted the boom keeping extension pressure, and it worked perfectly as we took our scheduled fuel load without any further problems. Since there were no reported malfunctions or recent maintenance work on our receptacle reported in the aircraft forms (AFTO 781), I rationalized that the problem was in the tanker's system and that we should continue.

As expected on this AR, when our gross weight gradually increased as we filled the tanks, we began to "over temp" the engines by exceeding the allowable continuous power settings. We signaled the tanker to begin a "toboggan", a simple maneuver where the tanker rolls-in 200-300 feet per minute descent on his autopilot. Now both aircraft are slowly flying downhill and the power required to stay on the boom is reduced to maintain the same airspeed. That worked as designed and we took as much fuel as we could pack in.

Our second (radio silent) AR was scheduled for 0530Z at a point 250 nm east of San Juan, Puerto Rico. Lt Col Bob Wenger moved in to fly the refueling from the (left) pilot's seat and I moved over to the (right) co-pilot's seat. (As an Instructor Pilot, I was equally comfortable and AR capable from either seat.) Other than the KC-135 tanker being 55 minutes late, the rendezvous, pre-contact and contact again went OK. Then it happened again, same problem with the latches. Again I made the decision to stiff-boom and signaled it to the boomer. And again we had to work a lot harder to get the fuel, including another toboggan.

There was no way that I was going to be a "no show" and fail our obligation for this important mission. Both of these AR's were critical, and I was prepared to do whatever was necessary to complete the fuel onload.

RECONNOITER THE POINT SALINES RUNWAY

The assigned initial task of our mission, and arguably the most important in terms of strategic intelligence value to the entire Urgent Fury mission, was to reconnoiter the Point Salines Airport runway to determine if it was clear of obstacles so that Special Operations and MAC Airlift C-130's could land. The less desirable alternative was for the C-130's to airdrop the Ranger battalions' personnel.

Once over the airfield at 0330 local, my intention was to minimize our sight and sound exposure by flying a maximum of two orbits at as high an altitude as possible. All external aircraft lighting would be off and we should not be visible from the ground against the black night sky. At our current altitude of 9000 ft the sound of our engines would be barely noticeable with directional perception not possible for anyone even paying close attention at this early hour.[1]

Figure 10. Point Salines Airport. Persistent cloud cover was a problem for getting high-quality pre-invasion pictures. The runway orientation is actually east-west. West is up in this picture. The runway is located on the narrow southwest tip of the island on the water.

A few miles west of the Point Salines airport, I slowed to orbit airspeed and configured the aircraft for flying orbit geometry, then proceeded eastbound to the airfield as both the TV sensor,

MSgt Luther Reece, and the IR sensor, SSgt Bob Anderson, scanned ahead. As we got closer, both sensors locked onto the runway giving me directional guidance to orbit directly above the airfield. The outline of the airfield area and the land/water boundary below were discernible through the pilot's heads-up display with only a few lights visible on the edge of the parking ramp area on the north side (in the picture, the parking ramp is obscured by clouds at mid-field).

I rolled into a loose orbit using Doppler (inertial) guidance leaving both sensors free to quickly scan up and down the runway. About half-way through the first orbit we went in and out of the bottoms of a cloud layer above us, and I had to descend slightly to stay clear. We were also intermittently in and out of light rain showers as we continued around.

Both sensor operators called the task completed before completion of the second orbit, so I rolled out and exited the area on a southerly course. We had been overhead the airfield less then six minutes total including the approach and exit, and left the area without any indications that we had disturbed anyone. The runway and general airfield environment remained dark - no AAA muzzle flashes, no tracers, and no searchlights.

As we departed the island, both sensor operators reported over the interphone that they had seen both large and small obstacles over the entire length of the runway. These included construction vehicles like bulldozers, trucks, road grading equipment, and many small obstacles like barrels and barricades. As we discussed what our report would be, the NAV, Capt Kirby Locklear, and the FCO, Lt Col Paul Wonderly, agreed with the sensor operators' evaluation that tactical C-130 landings on the Point Salines runway would not be possible due to runway obstructions. I then directed the FCO to make the call on the SATCOM Command Net to alert the airlift C-130 stream and the command elements of the airdrop requirement.[2]

DAY ONE

UHF SATCOM RADIO

Our UHF satellite communications (SATCOM) radio was set on the designated frequency for secure communications on the Command Net "A." The ABCCC aircraft, other mission aircraft (if capable), the various unit Command Posts, and other players were all on this net, and transmissions could be heard between the parties in a constant series of exchanges. For this mission I assigned our Electronic Warfare Officer (EWO), Lt George Williams, the additional duty to monitor this radio in case anything came up for us that required a response.

Also for use on Command Net "A" was a scheme for mission aircraft to report completion of key events that would enable commanders to track overall mission accomplishment. The planners designed an Execution Checklist that greatly simplified the notification process. Each event in the checklist had a brief event or situation description, a code word to denote completion, and the planned completion time.[3] When the task event or situation was actually completed, the code word and the time were transmitted on the Net by the accomplisher without further required explanation. Once acknowledged by ABCCC, the report was considered complete.

Prior to our departure from Hurlburt Field several problems were encountered with the FAX machine at the 2nd Air Division Command Post while trying to receive one complete execution checklist. Due to these problems, we departed without a complete checklist.[4]

We reported completion of our two air refuelings enroute, but the report of the status of the Point Salines Airport runway did not have a checklist line item so we had to use a clear text explanation.

Our further use of the checklist and our ability to monitor its completion was overcome by events (OBE) due to loss of the SATCOM. A short while after we had reconnoitered the Point Salines Airport runway and had completed the report to ABCCC on the net, the SATCOM radio failed, and we could neither transmit nor receive for the remainder of the Day-1 mission.

FORT JEUDY

Our second assigned task was to be overhead Fort Jeudy at H-Hour, 0500 local, to rendezvous with an unidentified ground party. Fort Jeudy is located on a peninsula 4 1/2 miles due east of the Point Salines Airport between the Calivigny/Egmont peninsula and the Westerhall peninsula. Neither the mission nor identity of the ground party had been briefed to us although we had a call sign and an assigned frequency. As we approached Fort Jeudy we continued to monitor the primary mission and intraplane UHF frequencies (and Guard channel). We heard some of the chatter from ABCCC and the MC/C-130 airlift stream carrying the Rangers as they approached the island.

We arrived overhead Fort Jeudy at 0450, two minutes before the lead MC-130 aborted the scheduled 0500 first airdrop at Point Salines. Shortly thereafter, the time for H-Hour was slipped by Colonel Bruce Fister, the Air Component Commander aboard ABCCC, to 0530 but we were already in orbit and committed, and could not assume that our ground party could know or do anything about a schedule slip.

As we rolled into orbit over Ft Jeudy at 6000 ft, we called the ground party on the assigned frequency and commenced a search for any persons or activity using both our IR and TV sensors. It was still dark and there was no activity below. As time went by we continued the search of the entire area and made repeated radio calls. No answer was received on the assigned frequency. Occasionally a bright searchlight in the vicinity of the city of St. George's trained on our orbit, but was too far away to really focus on our position. At 0515 we established communications with Lima 58 (Twiford) who was already in orbit either overhead or very near the Point Salines Airport.

We continued the search and made blind radio calls, but without answer. At 0530 (now dawn) the sky to the west lit up when the first airdrop was made and Lima 58 (Twiford) was firing at AAA defending the airport. We started to take 23mm AAA fired from the vicinity of St. George's approximately four miles to the northwest, but it was too far away to reach our altitude. At about 0545 we heard Lima 58 transmit that he was pulling off target with fire control problems and a hung 105mm round.

That call really got my attention! At that time I concluded that something was wrong with our planned rendezvous and our ground party was not going to show. We quickly departed the orbit to move west to the airport to support the Rangers. In retrospect, my timely decision limited the loss of our ineffective combat time to barely 15 minutes, although they were crucial minutes.

UNANSWERED QUESTIONS

No one has ever explained the reason for our assigned orbit over Fort Jeudy at H-Hour, and during my research I did not find any reference to that location or information about a mission there. The simplest answer would be that it was a leftover task from a previous plan that was changed and never cancelled. Another likely more complex scenario based on real facts with assumptions, although never briefed or assigned to us, is as follows:

1. Fort Jeudy had no significance whatsoever as a target. It appears that its single purpose was as a geographical parking location for an on-call gunship mission (Lima 56) that was in close proximity to the Calivigny peninsula.

2. The Fort Jeudy peninsula is the next peninsula to the east of the Calivigny/Egmont peninsula where the Calivigny Barracks cantonment is located. Calivigny Barracks was reported to be the PRA's main training camp and the peacetime home of the permanent battalion. Intelligence also claimed that it was the center of the Cuban military efforts on the island.[1] The cantonment was to be the objective of the forced march assault

by 2nd Battalion, 75th Infantry (Rangers) after landing on 25 Oct 1983. [2]

3. The ground party call sign and frequency were probably for the use of the advanced Ranger Battalion Forward Air Controller team that would lead the main Ranger force from Point Salines Airport to the assault on the Calivigny Barracks. The on-call gunship would provide armed reconnaissance and directional assistance as the force navigated along mostly unmarked back roads to the cantonment objective area.

4. This plan was overcome by events (OBE) when a stiff AAA defense at the airport strung out the landing sequence of both Ranger battalions. Consequently the attack on Calivigny Barracks was overcome by the fog of war, and the non-availability of the units and the timing of the actual events caused this mission to be postponed several days.

COME RUNNING TO POINT SALINES

As I rolled out on a westerly heading we remained configured and ready to roll-in and shoot any target. I pushed the airspeed up to 180 knots, expecting to be there in less than two minutes. As we got closer to the Point Salines airport, still level at 6000 ft, I could see ahead and slightly to the northeast of the airport in a small cluster of buildings (later identified as being in the town of Frequente) the muzzle flashes and smoke of a 23mm gun that appeared to be shooting in the general direction of Lima 58 (Twiford) but not coming anywhere close. A threat nonetheless, the 23mm had to be our first target.

I turned toward the muzzle flashes, directed both the TV and IR to the target's position, and called for the #1 gun (20mm). I quickly briefed the crew on what we were about to shoot as I followed fire control command guidance (on my flight instruments) to the target. Moments later as I rolled-in I commanded on the intercom, "Pilot's in the sight, arm the gun." The Flight Engineer, TSgt Glenn Gaudette, selected the "armed" position on the Master Arm switch and replied, "#1 gun is armed and ready." The target's position was immediately centered in the heads-up display (HUD) under the computed impact point (CIP) symbol, so I quickly fired a 5-second burst, followed by a short pause, then a 3-second burst. I could see the rounds from the first burst exploding on and all around the target, then rounds from the second burst hit. The 23mm stopped firing at us ... he's done!

The sensors confirmed a direct hit. "Pilot's out of the sight, safe the gun." In eight seconds at 2500 rounds per minute, we had delivered about 250-350 rounds of high-explosive ammo on the AAA gun crew's heads; they didn't have a chance. We'd hit and destroyed our first target with a lot more to go; elapsed time probably less than two minutes.

Figure 11. Looking northwest to the Point Salines runway and ramp. The control tower is barely noticeable at mid-picture to the far left. The Cuban construction worker's camp is on the hill just beyond the ramp.
Photograph courtesy of Rob Smith

After we cleared that first target, we orbited over the airport, still at 6000 ft, and contacted the Ranger ground FAC, call sign Delta 75, on the assigned frequency for more business. First we were directed to shoot several targets in succession, probably

12.7mm guns, still firing down on the Rangers. We fired 300 rounds of 20mm, 40 rounds of 40mm and 5 rounds of 105mm to destroy those targets.[1] We then were directed to fire on several buildings and troop positions up to one kilometer to the north of the runway and expended approximately 1000 rounds of 20mm, 100 rounds of 40mm, and 30 rounds of 105mm.[2] During this time Lima 58 (Twiford) returned to orbit 500 feet below us and also resumed shooting assigned targets on or near the airport.

Although the close air support (CAS) of Rangers on and around the Point Salines Airport was the primary focus of the gunships during the early hours on 25 Oct 1983, gunship activities began to include armed reconnaissance support for the same forces as elements of both Ranger battalions moved north and east from the airport later in the morning.

Over the next few days and until the AC-130 mission ended in early November, the task of providing 24/7 reconnaissance became the primary mission with few targets fired upon after the second day. The ground forces very quickly re-discovered the security value of the "eye in the sky" that could see ahead of their ground movements. They learned quickly that on-call immediate artillery support (sized to fit the target) was available just for the asking when they couldn't resolve the problem with their own small arms.

KC-10 AIR REFUEL

The operational planners for Operation Urgent Fury correctly recognized the need to provide on-scene Grenada air refueling support by KC-10 to extend the Spectre Gunship's on-station time. Without this support, effective gunship time over target would have been greatly reduced since the designated primary support base, Roosevelt Roads, Puerto Rico, was approximately two hours away.

At approximately 0730 it had been five hours since we last refueled and were close to Bingo fuel. Although we didn't want to leave orbit to air refuel, it was a good time to go since both

Lima 57 (Sims) and Lima 58 (Twiford) were both overhead PSA or in the vicinity, and actively working targets with the ground FAC. We cleared with the ground controller, de-configured from the firing mode, and departed the island.

As briefed, we turned westerly out over water maintaining 6000 ft and began a modified enroute rendezvous procedure. We called the KC-10 tanker on UHF (325.6 MHz) and advised him that we were proceeding to the 270 deg (radial) @ 50 nm, and in-the-block at 6000 to 8000 ft (as cleared by ABCCC). He answered immediately and within a few minutes appeared overhead. We were immediately cleared to the pre-contact position; it couldn't have been simpler or quicker.

Figure 12. KC-10 Extender air refueling tanker

Refueling from a KC-10 has always been a challenge as compared to a KC-135. The KC-10 generates more wake turbulence and "bad air", and generally requires higher engine power settings. Occasionally at higher gunship gross weights it becomes almost impossible to stay on the boom in level flight without exceeding maximum continuous engine power settings. The AC-130 is the worst case power-limited receiver with an abnormally high drag factor caused by all its external bumps and protrusions.

After a few minutes on the boom taking fuel, we got too heavy to maintain normal engine power settings. Intermittently

I began using power settings greater than the allowable in-flight continuous. I called for the tanker to "toboggan", and he rolled-in 200-300 feet per minute descent on his autopilot. Now we were both slowly going downhill, and my power available was enough to be able to maneuver as needed within the contact position envelope.

Much to my dismay the latch problem I had experienced during the two KC-135 refuelings showed up again. Now I just had to deal with it in this more severe situation. I popped off the boom a couple of times because I didn't quickly perceive and stop my rearward movement, and had to work even harder to get back on the boom and stay on.

We were done in approximately 30 minutes from start to finish, having onloaded approximately 30,000 lbs of JP-4. The KC-10 crew did an excellent job helping me to work around the latch problem.

One side benefit of being away from the shooting for a few minutes was that except for the pilots, the navigator, and the flight engineer, the rest of the crew had the opportunity to stand down and take a much needed break, the gun crew in particular. The gun crew is the most physically taxed during active firing since they're standing next to each gun to make it immediately available when called, and loading ammo in the gun when it's firing. Our lead gunner, SSgt John Eutzy, and his crew of SSgt Morris Blumenthal, SSgt Roger Betterelli, SSgt Bruce Grieshop, and SSgt Larry Hickey were the best. I called on them when I needed them, and they were superb! It seemed like all of the guns were always on the line and "Ready!" Surely not an easy feat to say the least, and one that kept them working very hard the whole time under very trying circumstances.

RE-TWEAK THE 105MM

By the time we returned to overhead PSA at 0815, the air-to-ground activity was beginning to slow down. Lima 57 (Sims) had returned from Calivigny, and Lima 58 (Twiford) had declared

Bingo and Winchester (i.e., out of usable ammunition), and had already departed for Roosevelt Roads.

We called the FAC for a target and were put on "standby" while he worked with Lima 57 (Sims). After this had gone on for about 15 to 20 minutes, it appeared that the delay could last a while longer. In the meantime we could probably re-tweak one of the guns and get back before we were called. Our 105mm, the #6 gun, had picked up a small error that kept us from getting direct hits. Given this opportunity, we decided to take a few minutes to go out and resolve that error. This would also refresh the air-to-surface ballistic wind setting that is stored and used for all the guns.

After clearing off with the FAC and ABCCC, we rolled out of the orbit and went out over water a few miles to the west. We cleared the area for ships, then threw out a Mark 60 flare carried for this purpose and went through the tweaking procedure. After firing a three-shot tweak at the floating flare with the 105mm, the computer calculated and stored new error "deltas" which were applied to the aiming point of future shots. One round fired for effect verified the accuracy of the new settings. We returned to overhead PSA to resume our standby status, which ended up lasting a little over one hour total.

Except for the rounds we used to tweak, the fact that we did not expend rounds from the other guns for that hour is probably one of the contributing reasons we still had ammo remaining at the end of the day. The other reasons are undoubtedly due to my personal conservative firing practice of shot quality over shot quantity, and lastly that this aircraft had an exceptional fire control computer and yielded good results on every round.

LITTLE HAVANA

As the Rangers started to move northeast from the airport, one of the first large pockets of resistance they encountered was the Cuban Mission Headquarters and "new camp" compound called Little Havana (not known to my crew by that name at the time), located about 1.8 km northeast of the airport terminal building. This compound was separate and distinct from the Cuban construction worker "old camp" located on the hill immediately behind the terminal building.

My crew (Lima 56) and Lima 57 (Sims) had been generally tasked to follow the forward progress of the Rangers, providing assistance by reconnoitering ahead of their advance and advising them of what was out there. Our TV and IR sensors could see what was ahead up the road but obviously could not discern any incoming ground fire until the FAC called it out. We moved up the road in a loose corkscrew flight path with the advancing Ranger leading elements.

As a small group of Rangers came up the access road to the east of the Little Havana compound they started to take heavy fire from its defenders. Both gunships picked up an orbit around the compound and passed to the FAC what we were observing as the Rangers returned fire.

The compound was fenced on all sides and about 50 x 75 yards in size with barracks and administration buildings clustered on the northern end, and a large open area near the southern end. In the southwestern corner was a fairly large bunker-like structure.

After a few minutes, the FAC, call sign Delta 75, advised us that they were communicating with the defenders in an effort to get them to surrender. Apparently the Cubans couldn't understand that their lives were in immediate danger with the two gunships overhead, so the FAC asked both of us to fire a couple of 105mm rounds in the open area and a single 105mm round into the bunker. Quite coincidentally we both fired on the bunker at exactly the same time and both were direct hits. The building totally exploded with a large ball of smoke and fire sending lumber and debris flying everywhere. We couldn't hear it but I'm sure it made a very large booming sound as well.

The firepower demonstration apparently had no effect, and again a few minutes elapsed as the surrender negotiations continued. The Cubans commenced fire again, and then started to run out of the barracks into the open area like they were on a cavalry charge, still shooting as they came out. The FAC reported to us that all hell was breaking loose and that they were starting to take heavier fire. He then cleared both of us to open fire before they came out of the gate and overran his position.

I had been maintaining firing geometry around the compound and was ready to shoot at anytime. The FCO announced to me, "pilot you are cleared to fire." I selected the #1 20mm gun and then directed, "Pilot's in the sight, arm the gun." The FE replied, "#1 gun is armed and ready." I rolled in with a dead aim on the running Cubans. As I slowly started to put thumb pressure on the firing button, the FAC screamed out on the radio, "they're surrendering, they're surrendering, cease fire, cease fire!" I stopped pressing and quickly commanded, "Pilots out of the sight, safe the gun!" I wiped away the sweat from my face and took a deep, deep breath with a sigh of relief.

The number of surrendering Cubans has been reported in books and the media to have been anywhere from 150 to 250. I still shudder when I think about how close they came to dying under a hail of bullets from above. During my interview with the Lima 57 Aircraft Commander, Lt Col Dave Sims, I asked him how close he was to firing and he said that he was within 2 to 3 seconds of pressing the firing button. I wonder if anyone ever told the Cubans how lucky they were to survive that day?

ATTACK ON FORT RUPERT

At 0945 we were directed to proceed to St. George's, the capital city of Grenada, to locate and attack Fort Rupert (aka Fort George). Fort Rupert sits atop the high ground on Fort George Point, the northern promontory guarding the harbor entrance to the city of St. George's. The fort was clearly marked on our "tourist" map.

When we arrived over the fort, the close proximity of the several surrounding buildings was recognized as a significant problem although the map contour lines indicated they were 100 to 150 feet lower than the fort's level. The large building about 200 yards to the south, about twice as large as the fort, was labeled as a hospital.

The structures we were directed to attack comprised the police headquarters atop the fort. It consisted of two two-story buildings, one on each of the south and east sides of a small courtyard about 60-75 feet across, and solid walls on the other two.

Figure 13. Battle damage to Ft Rupert from air attack on 25 Oct 1983

Two bastions on the fort's exterior corners outside the courtyard were clearly visible, one pointing south and one east. There was no indication that the target was defended, at least we didn't see anyone shooting at us. [1]

The hardened nature of this target clearly required use of the 105mm, and the need to minimize collateral damage to the surrounding buildings demanded pinpoint accuracy. I decided to shoot in the automatic, trainable mode where the guns move to train on the proper aiming point as directed by the TV or IR sensor through the fire control computer. This mode freed me to focus full-time on maintaining the firing orbit, virtually eliminating the need to stop shooting and re-acquire after every shot.

After firing two or three rounds at the target it was clear to me that the fire control computer was working perfectly using the new tweak data. We were getting direct hits or very near on every round which was what we needed, given the close proximity of the target to the surrounding buildings.

I was flying the orbits using command guidance to stay on geometry, making small corrections in bank angle as we went around the orbit. The TV and IR sensor operators took turns putting round after round right on the nose; it was like shooting fish in a barrel.

We worked over the courtyard, the inner face of the buildings and a few rounds through the roof of the main building. Altogether we fired about 25 rounds. Not one round landed outside the confines of the fort, and no casualties or collateral damage was reported. Clearly we had put the police headquarters out of commission, a fact that was confirmed several times in pictures and testimonials in post-war magazine articles and books. [2]

SEARCH FOR RICHMOND HILL PRISON

After we completed firing on Fort Rupert, the FAC directed us to find "Richmond Prison", reported to us to be in the city of St. George's and near the harbor. At that time we had never heard of the prison and had no knowledge of its significance. For reasons we will discuss next, the FAC could provide neither the map coordinates nor a description of the prison building. So we spent the next 15-20 minutes searching aimlessly for the prison, but couldn't find it.

Normally a gunship crew uses a 1:25,000 scale sectional chart that has a geographic grid depicting the longitude and latitude of the covered area. Consequently, any location on the chart can be referenced in terms of its geographic coordinates, and more importantly, these coordinates can be passed to another person or agency who can find the same exact location on their map.

At this small scale, detailed surface features such as highways, railroads, cities, rivers, towers, power lines, etc., along with contour lines and elevations are clearly depicted and named on the chart. This sized chart is perfect for target searches by comparing features on the chart with the actual surface features that can be seen outside the cockpit window. The gunship's NAV, FCO, TV and IR sensor operators would each have a copy that would have been studied and maybe annotated beforehand for the planned mission.

Figure 14. Ft Rupert and St. George's harbor looking southwest from Richmond Hill - Photograph courtesy of the author

Gunship crews did not have the normal sectional chart for use in Grenada. Instead a 1:50,000 scale map was issued that had neither geographic grid lines nor the necessary detail. What we got was a "tourist map" titled "Grenada: Island of Spice", 1979 edition, measuring 31" x 28" overall, with the entire island depicted in a 20" by 13" figure. The new Point Salines Airport was not even printed on the map; it was drawn in by hand. Most prominent buildings and geographic features were marked but smaller features and buildings were not. The map had two insets, one of the southwestern tip of the island at the 1:25,000 scale but not including the St. George's area, and the second a 6" x 8.5" blowup of St. George's inner city streets and harbor area. This map, issued to both gunship crews and the Army's ground and airborne forces, was totally inadequate for locating and shooting some less prominent targets and barely acceptable for the larger ones.

We searched the city and harbor area for the prison without positive results. The map problem and the guidance misdirection had undermined the whole search effort. In retrospect, we now know that "Richmond Hill" prison is not located in the city at all, but about 1.5 km to the east. Although the FAC had not assigned us to fire on the prison, even if we had found it we would have had a problem to do so for a couple of reasons. First, without the actual coordinates and/or a target description or photograph there was no way to positively identify the target, and gunships can't and won't shoot unconfirmed targets. Secondly, the prison was a building occupied by (unwilling) friendlies and a FAC must guarantee their safety. The weapons selected must be weighed between the need to drive off the defenders operating on the roof and ramparts while assuring the safety of the prisoners, presumably at the lower levels.

And lastly but still very important, our lack of prior knowledge of the prison is symptomatic of the larger problem caused by the highly compressed mission planning schedule that is described in almost every book or report written on the subject. That problem was that none of the gunship crews were briefed on the collateral plans to rescue occupants from Richmond Hill Prison or the Governor General's residence. Moreover, no gunships were tasked in advance to provide supporting firepower to either of those actions, a serious tactical mistake that may have contributed to the loss of life and the several casualties during the prison assault. Fortunately, the calls from the SEALs for gunship support at the Governor General's residence were made and answered in time to foil the assaults by People's Revolutionary Army (PRA) troops and their BTR-60 APC's, and the only loss of life was among those PRA forces.

(Author's Note: We sadly regret the loss of life of our Army helicopter colleagues and Special Forces brothers that we worked so closely with during the many training exercises dating back to the Iran Hostage Rescue mission in 1980. I would have jumped at the opportunity to be overhead (the properly identified) Richmond Hill Prison (RHP) to assist when their mission went down. I would have given the RHP defenders a little something more to think about instead of being able to hose those undefended helicopters. But sadly, that was not in the plan.)

GOVERNOR GENERAL'S RESIDENCE
RESCUE BECOMES TOP PRIORITY

An assault team from SEAL Team Six led by Lt Cmdr Duke Leonard had arrived by assault helicopter earlier on the morning of the 25th to secure the residence and protect the Governor General, Sir Paul Scoon, along with his family and staff. As the representative of Her Majesty's (Queen Elizabeth's) government, Sir Paul Scoon was recognized as the only bonafide authority around which a new Grenadian government could be formed.[1]

As the day wore on, Admiral Metcalf, Joint Task Force 120 Commander, declared that the protection and rescue of the Governor General's party became the top priority objective for all U.S. forces.[2] Admiral Metcalf later recounted, "But it soon became apparent, through talks with my State Department representatives, that this rescue was of paramount importance. In a political sense, the success of the entire operation now hung on the rescue of the governor general."[3]

Spectre gunships were the only air assets on-scene and on-call that could deliver the surgical firepower needed to do that job. Neither the 75th Rangers, nor the 82nd Airborne, nor the Marines had the ground assets or resources in position to stage a rescue until the morning of the 26th.[4]

DAY ONE

During the 24-hour local time period from 0700 on the 25th to 0700 on the 26th when the Governor General's party was finally liberated by Marine forces, each of the six gunships assisted at least once during their mission, and would spend an hour or so in orbit defending each time. Lima 57 (Sims) took the honors with the highest tally of three visits.

Fig 15. Gov Gen, Sir Paul Scoon

SUPPORT THE SEALS AGAINST THE PRA

After we completed the fire mission on Ft Rupert and could not find RHP, we were directed to the Governor General's residence almost next door (1 km) in St. George's. This was an urgent on-call task when the SEALs found themselves in a worsening situation that already had become extremely dangerous.

Unknown to us at the time, support for this mission had become the command element's top priority in terms of application of available offensive resources. We were not made aware of this task's importance. His residence and the Prime Minister's residence on Mount Weldale were occasionally referred to as Government House.

Grenadian People's Revolutionary Army (PRA) troops were in the immediate vicinity and on the residence grounds when the SEALs arrived and a firefight ensued as the team was inserted by two UH-60 Blackhawk helicopters. One of the helicopters was badly damaged as the SEALs fast roped down, and some in the team were wounded and remained on board along with some of their equipment, including the teams' SATCOM radio.[5]

Without the SATCOM radio link, the SEALs found themselves cutoff and unable to talk to anybody on the command network. The only other possible radio link they had was the MX-360, a hand held, line-of-sight, low power system exclusively used for intra-team communications and not compatible with anyone else's radios, even the gunship's. Luckily the team was able to use their MX-360 to establish contact to request gunship support thru their SEAL colleague's MX-360 on high ground at the Point Salines Airport five miles away. At the airport, their urgent fire support request was then passed to a Special Forces ground FAC, then to the gunship via VHF radio for an immediate supporting fire response.[6]

After arrival we searched out the advancing PRA troops and fired both 20mm and 40mm to push them back as directed by the SEALs. The attackers, however, continued to infiltrate from the Sans Souci and Gretna Green areas north and west of the Prime Minister's residence, and we were kept busy defending the Governor General's residence from being overrun. PRA troops made several more advances toward the residence but we forced them to retreat in a hail of gunfire.

DAY ONE

During several of the orbits we started intermittently picking up AAA coming from an area a mile or so to the northwest (later identified as 12.7mm in the D'Arbeau area). After temporarily moving our orbit to center on the AAA, a few rounds from the 20mm convinced them that it wasn't a good idea to fire on us. That was the end of that threat!

After about 15 to 20 minutes, Lima 57 (Sims) arrived to join us in the fray. I suspect that the heavy radio relay traffic between the SEALs and the gunship, and the high priority, prompted the JSOC command element aboard ABCCC to send the additional firepower. Shooting both 20mm and 40mm, Lima 57 (Sims) also attacked the advancing soldiers and then searched out and defeated small units hiding under the trees to the northwest of the residence. Eventually two BTR-60 armored personnel carriers (APC) arrived at the southeastern compound gate near the roundabout and were met by a hail of Lima 57's 40mm rounds. One was completely disabled and the other damaged but it quickly scurried away to hide.

After about another 30 minutes over Government House, we were down to Bingo fuel and had to leave station for Roosevelt Roads. Lima 57 (Sims) remained overhead for another 15 minutes until released and called to other targets. They would return later in the day after refueling at Barbados.

BINGO FUEL

When we reached Bingo fuel at approximately 1100 local, we had been airborne for 16.5 hours, the last 7.5 hours in full combat conditions. Lima 58 (Twiford) had already RTB'd to Roosevelt Roads, and Lima 57 (Sims) was still overhead at the Governor General's residence providing defensive support for the SEALs.

We again called for tanker support on UHF but got no response. At this time it was not clear whether the tankers were still on-station and available since our pre-mission flimsy didn't have a schedule of refueling window times. Without air refueling we had no choice but to RTB even though we still had limited stocks of ammo onboard.[2]

Although it didn't come into play, in the back of my mind I had a lingering concern for our ability to successfully stiff-boom air refuel a fourth time. We had beaten the odds when this operational emergency procedure worked for us three times before. If we hadn't been able to pull if off OK again, we would have no choice but to RTB anyway, and the fuel spent repeatedly trying could have jeopardized our safe recovery at Roosevelt Roads.

At this time we advised Lima 57 (Sims) that we were Bingo fuel and RTB. His transmitted response of "go to Barbados" without any additional information was very confusing to me, and I considered it to be non-directive. I recalled that only Roosevelt Roads (RR), not Barbados, was briefed as an authorized landing site, and after discussion in the cockpit mostly centered on the propriety of Barbados as a recovery airfield, I dismissed this option. We were unaware of any change to the briefed mission order, and Sims didn't say anything else to update us.[3]

Without any directions to the contrary, it was time for us to take it to the barn. The two hour, 434 nm leg to RR was quiet and uneventful. There were some really beat puppies on our airplane, especially the gun crew who had worked the guns and handled the ammunition while standing under 2-g conditions for almost the entire time. The normally chatty interphones up front and in the back were very, very quiet.

After two hours enroute we landed on runway 25 at RR. To our left on one of the inactive cross runways I saw several parked F-15's and AWACS aircraft, but didn't think anything about it at the time. As we taxied to parking near Base Operations, I received a message from ground control to call the Hurlburt Command Post (CP). I wonder what that's about.

As we walked into Base Operations, the Lima 58 (Twiford) crew was just leaving the desk after filing their flight plan to Barbados. They gave us the word about what was happening but I had to call the home CP anyway. "The war is not going very well, so we need for you to reposition to Barbados to fly more missions tomorrow. What's your maintenance status?" said the CP duty officer at Hurlburt. I told him we were OK and should get airborne within an hour or so. I ordered a fuel truck and sent word out to the plane not to unload luggage because we weren't staying. I guessed our crewmembers still at the airplane had probably figured that out when they saw Twiford and crew getting ready to leave.

By the time we filed our flight plan and got back to the plane, the downside effects of the 22-hour crew day and the continuous hours of extreme stress causing my system to release adrenaline, started to mess me up. I had started to relax a little from the tension of the day, and it looked like backing off was going to take me way down. After I got back aboard I could hardly focus or hold my eyes open, for the moment a physical basket case. Luckily our extra First Pilot, Lt Col Bob Wenger, was OK and had planned to fly the left seat to Barbados. All I could manage to do was to curl up on the floor behind the pilot's seat and fall asleep instantly. They woke me up as we landed in Barbados after a very quick two hour trip.

ARRIVE BARBADOS

We arrived at Grantley Adams International Airport, Barbados, after a two hour flight from Puerto Rico. I wasn't sure how the civilians were going to react to our "guns", but Lima 58 (Twiford) had landed before us and nobody seemed to care that now they had a second warbird on the field. Mixing commercial airliners and AC-130's just seemed a bit awkward to me with a lot of gawking tourists peering out of the passenger terminal windows trying to figure us out as we taxied past.

At this time I thought our two gunships were the first mission airplanes to come into Barbados. I was not aware that Lima 57 (Sims) had refueled here, and that a lot of Military Airlift Command (MAC) C-5 and C-141 traffic had been through in the preceding 24 hours, including those that offloaded the Army's UH-60 assault helicopters.

Its one of those things where you don't know what you don't know until you find out after the fact. The in-flight failure of my SATCOM system had a far more deleterious effect than I ever suspected, causing us to miss a lot of operational details, and especially how the war was going.

Ground control parked us on Red ramp in front of the old terminal building next to the other gunship. After shutdown, filling out the forms, offloading luggage, and locking the bird for our crew rest, a civilian vehicle arrived to take us to contract quarters. The other crew had apparently already gone into crew rest. I asked some of the flight line workers if any Air Force personnel were there that I could talk to, but couldn't find anyone who knew anything about our operations. Usually at a non-military airfield someone will meet an incoming crew and take them to talk to some U.S. military point of contact on the airfield. Seems I had struck out on this one; we seemed to be on our own. (As we know now the FOB personnel were already there, but it's not known why they didn't meet us to provide operational crew support.)

I got from the driver the name of the hotel where we would be staying, the Blue Horizon at Rockley Beach, and I sent the rest of the crew to the hotel. I had to call the Hurlburt CP to let them know I had arrived and to get the "plan" for tomorrow. I finally found a phone in a small flight line maintenance shack and got through to the Command Post after a few minutes.

The CP Duty Officer said that a C-141 with another 16th SOS crew, Maj Larry Strelau as the Aircraft Commander, and a gunship maintenance contingent would be landing Barbados in about an hour. The plan was for my crew to come out of crew rest the next morning at 1000, takeoff for Grenada at 1300 and stay on station there as long as possible, then return to Barbados. Our takeoff time was sequenced with Lima 58 (Twiford) to allow for extended coverage rather than all leave at the same time. Lima 57 (Sims) was at Roosevelt Roads and would remain overnight (RON) there and come to Barbados in the morning.

I assumed someone had a plan to get ammunition for these next day's missions, but it wasn't clear how that would happen. We hadn't shot nearly as much as the other two crews and had about 1500 20mm, 125 40mm, and 50 105mm (slightly less than 1/2 of a normal combat load) remaining after starting with extra ammunition for all guns.

I decided to wait around for the C-141 arrival to greet both the incoming crew and the maintenance team. When they arrived, Colonel "Robbie" Robertson, the wing Deputy Commander for Maintenance, was commanding a small team of about 15-20 maintainers who only had their personal toolboxes.

This bunch had been alerted and deployed from Hurlburt as a quick reaction response without the larger maintenance support kits. Unfortunately, they could not bring any ammunition on board the aircraft with the crew and maintenance personnel. The plan was for the rest of the team to arrive the next day along with maintenance's War Readiness Spares Kit (WRSK) and a complete shipment of ammunition.[1, 2]

After talking with the new crew for a while and debriefing maintenance on our flyable status, the plan changed. Maj Strelau and crew would fly my airplane on an immediate sortie with my residual ammunition and supplement the 105mm load from Twiford's unused rounds. I gave them a thorough operations crew briefing with the maps and handouts still on board, to include frequencies, call signs, what to expect and generally everything they needed to fly the mission.

With that briefing done it was time for me to call it a day. Except for the two hour nap earlier that afternoon, it had been almost 36 hours since I had slept between the sheets. I certainly didn't have any trouble sleeping that night except that it took a long time to unwind and fall asleep as the day's events went round and round in my head.

[Author's Note: Some things you only learn about after 25 years, and are very happy you didn't know about it at the time. The tale I heard is that after my crew checked in at the hotel (without me), they all got very hungry and thirsty, what else?

After enjoying a libation while sitting around the hotel pool visiting with "friendly tour guides", they found a small cantina down the street and went in for a bite, still dressed in their "combat attire" to include survival vests with .38's still in the holsters. (Since there was no official government agency to meet us at the airport, there was no place to check the weapons and the survival vests, so we were required to keep them on our person at all times.) They really had a good time drinking rum and eating chili in the midst of casually dressed vacationers, and were the only diners in the place "packing heat!"]

NOTES - CHAPTER 2

AT THE AIRCRAFT

1. The crew position title of Illuminator Operator (IO) was a carryover from the Vietnam days when there was a piece of equipment onboard they had to operate in addition to performing loadmaster and scanner duties. Although that equipment was no longer on the aircraft in the 1980's, the IO position title remained unchanged. I understand that now (2010) the IO position title has been changed to Loadmaster (LM).
2. 8th Special Operations Squadron, Historical Report 1 Jul – 31 Dec 1983, 4.
3. Lima 57 and Lima 58 had different combinations of extra 20mm and 40mm ammunition. I could not find any consistency in the combinations or reasons for the differences.

TAKEOFF FROM HURLBURT

1. Rider 10 was our call sign for use with Air Traffic Control until we got out of controlled airspace later in the flight. For all tactical operations, including air refueling, and the remainder of the mission we used the mission call sign Lima (lee-ma) 56.
2. Collette Interview, 8 Mar 2007.

ENROUTE AIR REFUEL

1. Technical Order 1C-130(A)H(I)-1 , page 4-378, Boom Receptacle.

RECONNOITER THE POINT SALINES RUNWAY

1. The minimum exposure value of a quick in-and-out was paramount to me at this time. As far as I knew, not having been briefed otherwise,

the defenders did not know we were coming later in the morning and I didn't want to be the one to give them a wakeup call.

2. For their own reasons, several authors writing on Urgent Fury have taken the liberty of assigning additional purposes to my runway reconnoiter task. These include: dropping Ranger pathfinder parachutist, searching for AAA installations, and mapping out enemy troop positions to decide where to airdrop on the airfield. My reply is: 1) Gunships don't airdrop paratroopers, that's not our job, don't have room aboard for non-aircrew, and we're not trained for that task. 2) Knowing if AAA was employed at the airfield would have been valuable information for planning purposes, but at this time and in this situation we've already committed to assuming that AAA is there, and there's nothing more we can do about it, and 3) Aside from the fact that locating enemy troop positions would require a lot more overhead time, and better done from a lower orbit altitude, the accuracy of an airdrop is not assured even under the best of conditions. The greatest concern for the upcoming airdrop was to avoid dropping the overloaded Rangers in the water which in some places was a hazard on both sides of the runway. The water on the north side of the runway was the remaining part of an inlet that was partially filled in to build the runway across its southern end.

3. Carney, *No Room for Error*, 144.

4. *2nd Air Division After Action Report*, 130.

FORT JEUDY
1. Adkin, *Urgent Fury*, 279.
2. Ibid., 278.

COME RUNNING TO POINT SALINES
1. *History of the 2nd Air Division*, 135.
2. Ibid.

ATTACK ON FORT RUPERT
1. Post war photos clearly show ZU-23 guns sited on both the northeast and southeast bastions that were not evident to our sensors from 6000 ft. The guns were likely abandoned when our attack began giving us at least two "functional kills."
2. Adkin, *Urgent Fury*, 288.

BINGO FUEL
1. In a post-operation interview with Brigadier General Robert B. Patterson, 21st Air Force Vice Commander, assigned by HQ MAC as the Operation Urgent Fury Commander of Airlift (COMALF), he

responded in part to the question about MAC aircraft having to air refuel by saying "… , and a few C-141s got the opportunity to 'hit' the tankers. Primarily the special operations birds benefited." Although we had been briefed that tankers were on-call and available exclusively for the special operations aircraft, his statement raises the possibility that maybe the on-call tanker was busy refueling C-141's on another frequency, or perhaps had RTB'd Roosevelt Roads to refuel, and that is why they did not respond. Tanker information was requested through FOIA but not made available to clear up this point.

2. As it turned out, our residual ammo when combined with Maj Twiford's 105mm rounds enabled the sortie by Maj Strelau's crew (using our call sign, Lima 56, and our aircraft, 69-6575) after we transited Roosevelt Roads and recovered at Barbados. Our bird, 69-6575, was Fully Mission Capable (FMC), and Twiford's aircraft, 69-6573, was Not Mission Capable (NMC) because of an inoperative Fire Control Computer and #6 gun broken breech block.

Maj Strelau's sortie over the Governor General's residence well after dark was key to the continued support of the SEALs by surprising the PRA troops and keeping them at bay. No other ammo for gunships was available at Barbados until the follow-on gunships arrived with full or partial ammo loads onboard later in the evening.

3. Later I learned that our Wing Commander, Col Hugh L. Hunter was aboard Lt Col Sims' aircraft. I suspect that Col Hunter was busy on the SATCOM Command Net at that time trying to sort out with mission commanders what the requirement for gunships would be in a yet unplanned follow-on response to the continuing stiff PRA and Cuban resistance. If necessary he could certainly have countermanded my decision to RTB Roosevelt Roads at that time, or relayed a divert directive through ATC, but he did not.

GOVERNOR GENERAL'S RESIDENCE

1. Adkin, *Urgent Fury*, 113.
2. Kulielski, *Grenada: Five Years Later*, A-12.
3. Ibid.
4. Gormly, *Combat Swimmer*, 221.
5. Ibid., 220.
6. Ibid., 221.

ARRIVE BARBADOS

1. Colonel Robertson interview, 17 Apr 2007.

2. Both Major Don Kemper (Lima 59) and Capt David Tarpley (Lima 61) arrived Barbados during the night with more than a full combat load between them. These stocks resolved the immediate ammunition problem for missions on the morning of the 26th. A C-141 with the full ammunition shipment and WRSK arrived from Hurlburt Field on the 27th.

CHAPTER 3
DAY TWO & MOP UP

AIRBORNE BATTLEFIELD COMMAND & CONTROL CENTER (ABCCC)

Fig 16. EC-130E Airborne Battlefield Command & Control Center aircraft

One of the least known and least recognized players on the Grenada rescue mission was the Airborne Battlefield Command and Control Center (ABCCC), an EC-130E Hercules aircraft specially modified and equipped to provide military commanders and the National Command Authority with on-scene command-and-control and communications support. ABCCC aircraft flew 44 employment phase sorties for 248.3 hours during Operation Urgent Fury, 24 Oct - 9 Nov 1983, in support of Joint Task Force (JTF) 123.[1] During that time, ABCCC had the authority to scramble the AC-130H Spectre gunships and to coordinate live close air support missions for both the AC-130s and the Navy A-7s.[2] It is most appropriate that their story be included here.

Two ABCCC (pronounced A-B-triple-C) aircraft were orbiting just offshore south of the island and slightly above the gunships' altitude when the first MC-130 dropped its load of Rangers at 0530 local time (H-Hour) on 25 Oct 1983.[3] On board the first ABCCC (62-1825) commanded by Lt Colonel James Williams, were the JTF123 command element from the HQ Joint Special Operations Command (JSOC), Ft Bragg NC, consisting of the Commander, Major General Richard Scholtes (USA), Call Sign -Viking, and the Air Component Commander, Colonel Bruce Fister (USAF), Call Sign - Golf 95. On board the second ABCCC (62-1818) commanded by Captain John Carkeet, were the Deputy JTF123 Commander, Colonel Bill Palmer (USA), and the Deputy Air Component Commander, Lt Col Jim Schenk (USAF).[4]

The two ABCCCs had flown down from Pope AFB, NC, with one air refueling each from a KC-135 in the same airspace but not in the same stream as the airlift aircraft. The MC-130's and the airlift C-130's using station keeping (SKE) formation procedures carried the 1st and 2nd Battalions of the 75th Infantry (Ranger) Regiment, from Fort Stewart GA and Fort Lewis WA, respectively. These two units, both specially trained in airfield seizure, were tasked to either airdrop or airland, as required, to capture the Point Salines Airport located on the southwestern tip of Grenada.

Unfortunately as the aircraft approached the airport drop zone (DZ) for an 0500 (still dark) time-on-target, un-forecasted moderate rain showers and thunderstorms, intermittent low ceilings and reduced in-flight visibility, combined with navigation equipment failure aboard the lead MC-130, caused a "no drop" situation for safety reasons. Without the ability to measure the in-flight wind velocity and direction for computing the air release point, and with the narrow DZ with water on one side (on both sides at the DZ midpoint), it was correctly declared to be an unsafe situation. Even the slightest drop error there could cause multi-personnel loss of life because these extremely heavily laden paratroopers ready for combat could not survive a landing in the water.[5] The aborted airdrop required the Air Component Commander aboard the lead ABCCC to quickly sort out the problems and re-synchronize the airdrop schedule for a 0530 drop with a different lead aircraft.[6]

During the first re-scheduled 3-ship airdrop pass at 0530, 23mm and 12.7mm AAA batteries on the hills north of the airport opened fire. The lead aircraft continued to make its airdrop, but the horrendous AAA tracered rounds and airbursts caused numbers two and three aircraft in the formation to abort their drop and breakout over water to the south.[7] This potentially dangerous turn of events required another immediate massive reorganization plan for the entire stream while the AC-130H Spectre gunships were overhead defeating the AAA. The remaining C-130's were re-directed away from the airport by ABCCC to several different holding patterns at stacked altitudes.[8]

As the delay wore on and minutes passed, dwindling onboard fuel supplies became a major concern.[9] The airdrops finally resumed at 0552 and continued until 0700. At 0735 the airfield was secured, and the landings to offload non-droppable personnel, vehicles and equipment were completed between 0737 and 0755. Also needing fuel while on-station during the morning, both ABCCC aircraft were able to air refuel from the on-call KC-10.

The Air Component Commander on the ABCCC Battle Staff, Col Bruce Fister, received laudatory Kudos from Colonel Hugh Cox, Commander, 2nd Air Division, Hurlburt Field, FL (parent unit of the MC-130s and AC-130s), for his quick and decisive handling of this otherwise catastrophic situation.[10] The on-scene presence of an authoritative command and control function that quickly adapted to resolve the mission threatening factors clearly made the difference in keeping the assault plan on track. Maintaining control of the airlift resources and executing a successful alternate plan led to the ultimate success of the airdrop mission, albeit delayed but without major mishap or casualties.

Shortly after the Point Salines Airport was secured by the Rangers at 0735, both aircraft landed to offload their JSOC passengers and a team of ABCCC communications NCOs to help setup JSOC's command radios at their Field Command Post.[11] After only a short ground time, both aircraft departed and resumed their on-station orbits.

During the morning the lead ABCCC worked the search and rescue (SAR) of the crew from the Blackhawk helicopter that was heavily damaged during the assault on Richmond Hill Prison.[12] It had crashed at Amber Belaire, a sparsely populated residential community on the small peninsula about one mile east of the Point Salines airport. The co-pilot had reported 13 on board, 8 ambulatory, and needed help. Ranger and Delta personnel fast-roped down from the escorting Blackhawk, and gunship Lima 57 (Sims) suppressed the gunfire coming across the water from the True Blue peninsula to the east.[13] They also drove off the approaching PRA troops moving south down the road from the village of Ruth Howard. ABCCC finally located and tasked a Navy helicopter to assist with crew pickup and transport.[14] At about mid-morning, all were flown directly to the USS Guam amphibious assault ship (Admiral Metcalf's flagship) where the injured received immediate medical treatment.

At the end of their Day-1 mission, both ABCCCs recovered at Grantley Adams Airport, Barbados, only about 30 minutes away. The crews began flying a daily schedule out of Barbados to maintain 24/7 coverage over Grenada. The missions usually began with a landing at Point Salines to pickup an Army Ground Liaison Officer (GLO) and to key-up the cryptographic equipment to enable secure communications.[15] One of these stops was particularly exciting when the outside scanner heard two shots land close by as he was standing on the ramp. As he jumped back aboard a loud "ping" was heard near the tail by the entire battle staff; the aircraft made a hasty takeoff.[16] On other missions ABCCC was asked to transport individuals to Barbados, one a wounded Grenadian civilian with an IV in place who had been caught in a fire fight where his wife and daughter had been killed.[17]

A third ABCCC aircraft (62-1857) was dispatched from Keesler AFB to join the first two at Barbados on 27 Oct 1983, and landed there after refueling at Roosevelt Roads and flying a four hour mission on-station at Grenada. Since each flight crew was augmented with extra crewmembers to permit an extended crew day for the Day-1 missions, a fourth crew was created with some of the extras to enable an 8 hour on, 24 hours off flight schedule for the next two weeks. Like the gunship crews, the ABCCC flight crews and battle staffs were billeted in "nice" hotels located either on or directly across the street from the beach. The record does not show if any complaints were received about the billeting arrangements.

Like the gunship crews, the ABCCC crews used the old terminal building on the flight line at the Barbados airport as their base of operations. Both units had a small operations desk there to take care of crew scheduling, day-to-day operational communications and as a focal point for coordinating with the maintenance teams. There was also a small café immediately behind the terminal serving light meals and where the crews could fill the coffee and water jugs for the onboard galley.[18] MAC also had an Airlift Control Element (ALCE) operations desk in the same area with an operating UHF radio that enabled direct contact with inbound and outbound aircraft.

Both the 7th Airborne Command and Control Squadron (ACCS) at Keesler and the 1st Special Operations Wing (SOW) at Hurlburt Field, deployed maintenance teams to support their TDY aircraft. The 7th ACCS Maintenance Officer, Lt Colonel Ron Ziebold, commanded a small contingent of only 10-15 maintainers. He was an old friend of the 1st SOW Maintenance Officer, Colonel Robbie Robertson, who commanded a larger team of about 40 maintainers with a maintenance WRSK Kit consisting of spare parts and specialized tools. Colonel Robertson was former commander of the 7th ACCS from 1980-83, and was well acquainted with the 7th's crews and aircraft.

Some mutual consolidation of effort, cross-unit support, and combined resources resulted in record consecutive on-time mission departures and an extremely high reliability rate for both units under difficult circumstances.

During the early part of the Day-1 mission on 25 Oct 1983, the gunships worked directly with the Ranger Battalion Air Liaison Officer (ALO) and Ranger Company Forward Air Controllers (FAC) for direct fire on Close Air Support (CAS) and Troops-In-Contact (TIC) missions. As the day wore on and the Ranger close air support requirements at and near the Point Salines airport subsided, more communications traffic with the gunships was handled by the Ground Liaison Officer (GLO) aboard ABCCC, particularly in conjunction with targets north of the airport and in and around St. George's. Once the Joint Special Operations Command (JSOC) command element established a command position on the airport in the partially completed new terminal, their main communications link was primarily through the ABCCC to the gunships. After the 82nd Airborne Division was fully in-place on the 27th, the JSOC command element and both of the Ranger Battalions folded their tents and began departing for home station. All requests for gunship fire support and reconnaissance missions were then coordinated through the GLO aboard ABCCC.

GRAND ANSE BEACH

On 26 Oct 1983, Day-2 of the mission, Lima 56 (Couvillon) departed Barbados at 1302 local time, and arrived on-station Point Salines 38 minutes later. The FAC gave us two target assignments for the impending operation to rescue the St. George's University (SGU) medical school students at the Grand Anse Beach complex. Our targets were the Carifta cottages and the Police Training College building, both immediately adjacent to the beach area and clearly marked on our "tourist" map. The A-7's from the USS Independence would also participate to attack the Police Training College building.

Our first assignment was to shoot each of the Carifta Cottages in advance of the rescue mission. The cottages, about 40 total, were arranged along the edges of an (estimated) 700 yard long rectangular field slightly south of the east-west beach road and just across the street from the SGU Medical School Grand Anse Complex (the driveway can be seen mid-picture left in Fig. 17) I selected the 20mm for these soft targets and started shooting with #1 gun. After firing a 2 to 3 second burst into each cottage I shifted my aim to the next and continued. About halfway through, I switched to the #2 gun so as to balance the remaining 20mm ammunition between the two guns. I can't recall seeing anyone run from the cottages, but I think it's fair to say that any remaining occupants are no longer with us!

Fig 17. (left) Carifta cottages at Grand Anse. Fig 18. (right) Two cottages burned to the ground. Photographs courtesy of Kevin Palush

For a few minutes while we were shooting the cottages, an A-7 was simultaneously working over the Police Training College buildings. Each time he came around in his racetrack pattern to shoot his cannon or drop bombs, we would use our "cease fire" safety procedure, and then continue shooting when he was clear. The person who planned this attack certainly didn't think clearly about the safety issues of having two dissimilar weapons platform working separate targets within a few yards of each other, and how the firing orbits and firing passes might overlap.

After we finished with the cottages and the A-7 had departed, I moved the sensors and shifted the orbit to the Police Training College building since it didn't look like the A-7 had done much damage. Because this target was fairly hard and I wanted to avoid any collateral damage to the nearby medical school buildings, I selected the 40mm gun.

Figure 19. Police Training College at Grand Anse Beach

The 40mm gun was my favorite. I called it the "gentleman's gun" and I could drive nails with it. Usually when I fired the 40mm gun, I trimmed the aircraft (rudder and aileron) real tight so it would tend to stay close to nominals by itself, then I tightened up the computer (symbol) coincidence and rate to the lowest available "one and one" setting. Three to five second bursts with direct hits were the norm. The sound in the cockpit of the gun shooting is a soft "boom, boom, boom" with only the slightest perceptible aircraft side movement from the gun's recoil. We put over 150 rounds into that building and didn't miss. Parts of the building were burning when we were done.

The 105mm would have been a better choice for that target, but safety considerations compelled us to use the smaller gun to limit the shrapnel field and possible collateral damage. The medical school complex buildings were less than 150 meters away, marked as a friendly position with white sheets on the dormitory building's roof. When possible we restricted our firing in segments of the orbit to avoid ricochet in the direction of the medical school complex.

During the last few orbits, a AAA gun located about ½ km northeast of the school campus (within our orbit) came up and started shooting at us intermittently. We quickly moved the sensors over to the expected location and found a 12.7mm bunkered gun.[1] We fired about 30 rounds of 40mm in the trainable mode, and that silenced him.[2] He didn't come up again.

We ceased firing at the scheduled end time and monitored the main force of Marine CH-46's and CH-53's as they came in over the water to land the Rangers on or very near the beach. The helicopter extraction of the students appeared to go very well and it was over in about 30 minutes.

The remainder of our mission that day continued with armed reconnaissance support for the Rangers and the 82nd Airborne troops as they continued moving northeast toward the capitol St. George's. We departed at 1930 and landed at Barbados 40 minutes later. Our mission over Grand Anse Beach turned out to be the last time our crew fired the guns over Grenada.

UNCONTROLLED A-7s

While firing on the various targets on both the 25th and 26th, it was not unusual for a Navy A-7 (or a flight of two) from the USS Independence to fly uncontrolled within the ground track of our firing orbit and below our altitude. The first time it happened was a big surprise and really got our attention. That kind of thing is not supposed to happen in a semi-controlled environment, but not everyone plays by the rules. Sometime these aircraft were just passing through, while other times they would be striking their own ground target on repeated passes, totally oblivious to our presence. Needless to say, this could be very dangerous situation for the A-7 if we did not see him first and use extra safety precautions.

Early on the first day it became apparent that this situation would come up from time to time, and so we had to work out a crew coordination procedure to provide for safety. The procedure we adopted involved using the augmenting crew members on board (i.e., the extra pilot, navigator, and flight engineer) to provide the extra eyeballs added to the right scanner and IO already scanning outside the aircraft. One extra crewmember would stand behind the pilot and one behind the copilot scanning outside the cockpit windows in addition to the right-side and rear scanners (IO). If at any time during the firing orbit another aircraft intruded below our firing orbit airspace, or appeared that he was going to intrude, any crewmember seeing the intruder would call "cease fire" and the reason. The guns were safetied until the airspace below us was clear. We also found that verbalizing the direction and path of the intruder made the procedure work more smoothly and gave each crewmember a better real-time sense of when it was going to be safe to fire and when it wasn't.

The best example of this situation happening to my crew was on the 26th when we worked the targets at Grand Anse. We were shooting the Carifta Cottages and an A-7 was shooting the Police Training building at the same time and only a few hundred yards apart. We handled it exactly as we had practiced and the A-7 wasn't in danger at any time, but he made everybody happy when he pulled off the target and departed for the carrier.

THIS ONE WILL CURL YOUR HAIR

The scariest story involving A-7s was told to me by Maj Don Kemper (Lima 59). On a particular mission they were supporting the 82nd Airborne in the Prickly Bay peninsula area. Under control of the 82nd FAC, Kemper's crew was shooting the 40mm at a building housing enemy troops when a flight of two A-7s came up from his six o'clock position and flew right through his Head's Up Display aiming line to the target and well below his orbit altitude. He immediately ceased fire.[1]

The rapid-fire stream of single 40mm rounds going down to the target luckily missed them, but what if he had been firing the 20mm guns instead. If you've ever seen tracered 20's fired at night you'd know that 20's make virtually a solid stream of bullets between the gunship and the target. Anything flying in the airspace directly in that path between the gunship and the target is DEAD!

Neither ABCCC nor the FAC was working the A-7s, nor did the A-7s answer Lima 59's call on the UHF radio Guard Channel that all aircraft are required to monitor. The A-7s came through his target area twice more, again uncontrolled and oblivious to Lima 59's presence, and he again used the same type of safety procedure to finish his mission. Bagging a pair of A-7's would have ruined everybody's day!

MOVE TO ROOSEVELT ROADS

By 26 Oct 1983, ramp space saturation at the already busy Grantley Adams International Airport, Barbados began to be a significant problem for their airfield management, and our gunship operation was causing a lot of it (not to even mention the three ABCCC aircraft). By then we had increased to six aircraft, requiring a lot of permanent aircraft parking and more ramp space for extended maintenance operations.

The directed solution was to split the gunship operation between Barbados and Roosevelt Roads, Puerto Rico (RR). So after we returned to Barbados from our mission in the early morning hours of 27 Oct, our crew was directed to move operations to RR. We arrived there before dawn and checked into the base's visiting officer and visiting non-commissioned officer quarters.

This change also affected our mission profile by adding extra flying time to each sortie. The Barbados based aircraft would fly six-hours on station and return to Barbados, and the Puerto

Rico based birds would fly four-hour on station then stop at Barbados for fuel on the return flight to Puerto Rico. By then the KC-135 and KC-10 air refueling support was no longer available.

The second problem (and one included in the After Action Lessons Learned list), and perhaps one more significant than the first, was the requirement to also split maintenance support. It seems that manning levels for deployed operations don't include enough specialists for dual basing. So trying to operate that way is like shooting yourself in the foot.

Figure 20. Second from left: Lt Col Bob Wenger, AFSOB Officer, receives an Intel briefing

Within the next couple of days Lt Col David Sims, the aircraft commander of Lima 57 and also our incoming 16th Special Operations Squadron Commander designate, had organized the mission schedule so that each of the six aircraft would fly on a rotating schedule to provide 24/7 coverage. The outgoing aircraft departed station after the incoming aircraft received the handoff briefing on the air-to-air company frequency. Each aircraft was fully armed to provide armed reconnaissance and close air support to the 82nd Airborne troops and the Marines as they cleared pockets of resistance and completed the general mopping-up operation.

On 28 Oct 1983, Lt Col Bob Wenger was pulled from our crew (Lima 56) to function as the Air Force Special Operations Base (AFSOB) Officer until he redeployed with our crew (see Figure 20). The AFSOB functioned as focal point for our 1st Special Operation Wing assets to interface with tasking agencies.[1] As senior officer, Col Robbie Robertson remained the deployed unit Commander.

On 27 Oct 1983, Capt Bob Hockman and a non-tactical minimum crew ferried the sixth gunship from Hurlburt to Barbados to be flown as needed on the scheduled missions. When Lt Col Sims later moved into the AFSOB officer position, Capt Hockman assumed the Aircraft Commander position of Sims' Lima 57 crew, and the rest of Hockman's ferry crew (i.e., Hoesen, Collette, Franco, Stone, and Gowdy) moved to Capt Tarpley's (Lima 61) crew to bring it up to full augmented strength.

CAPTURE OF GENERAL HUDSON AUSTIN

On Sunday, 30 Oct 1983, we flew our third recce mission over Grenada but the first from our base at Roosevelt Roads. This was the first of three that we flew as part of the 24/7 continuous coverage effort that the gunship contingent was to provide to 82nd Airborne and Marine units until cessation of hostilities on 2 Nov.

We arrived on-station shortly after 1200 local. At mid-afternoon we got a call from the 82nd Airborne ground FAC requesting support for a planned operation at Westerhall Point, an up-scale housing area on the Westerhall peninsula located five miles east of Point Salines Airport. The plan called for "eye-in-the-sky" support for the paratroopers as they searched house-to-house to capture several high-ranking Grenadian Revolutionary

Military Council (RMC) officers who were known to be hiding in that area.

The operation started and completed without a hitch. From our vantage point it appeared that the troops made quick work of the capture, apparently without firing a shot. Although we didn't know the identity of the persons captured at the time, other than they were persons of extreme interest, we later learned that one of them was General Hudson Austin, the leader of the Grenadian Revolutionary Military Council (RMC), and the others were some of his council cronies.

At the end of the four hour mission, we were relieved by another gunship and returned to Roosevelt Roads after a refueling stop at Barbados. Over the next several days we flew two more of this type of mission, with our last one flown in the early morning hours of 2 Nov 1983.

NAMING THE GRINDER

After we had flown several missions with tail number 69-6575, the same aircraft we flew in from Hurlburt originally on the 25th, we began to get attached to the old bird and started regarding it as our personal aircraft. Being able to fly the same bird on every flight while TDY was very unusual, especially if it was in good shape and likely to be "stolen" for other crew's missions. Keeping the same tail number especially made it a lot easier to keep up with the maintenance status and to accept and fly with write-ups (i.e., maintenance discrepancies that require corrective action) that might otherwise be found objectionable. You just learn to live with an old friend's bumps and bruises.

About this time I was also noticing the cohesiveness of this aircrew after we had flown several particularly challenging missions together and they had performed superbly. They were identifying themselves with the claim of being the "best" crew, particularly when talking war stories with members of other crews. I was even told that sometimes the claims had something to do with the post-mission partaking of liquid refreshment on the beach in the spirit of good fellowship. Rumors of that kind can be vicious!

ANY AIRPLANE FLOWN BY THE BEST SPECTRE CREW HAS GOT TO HAVE NOSE ART!

Being an avid WW II buff and recalling the many pictures of combat aircraft with nose art, I decided that we needed nose art too, and came up with the idea of naming "our" bird and how it would add to the crew identity. The idea of putting "Grenada" in the name had a particular ring to it, but we needed an applicable action word that started with a "G" to provide an alliterative sound. Well, after a few crew suggestions that I didn't care for (X-rated material was not allowed), I made a command decision and decided on "Grenada Grinder." We had certainly done a lot of target grinding.

Before the next mission, our two Flight Engineers, TSgt Glenn Gaudette and SSgt Fernando "Chico" Daleccio, (the best two FE's in the business) scrounged cans of florescent orange and white spray paint and painted "Grenada Grinders" on the nose above the TV sensor opening (aka crew entrance door). They added the extra "s" to indicate the plurality of the crew members, and I guess that's OK. They also painted white symbols shaped like outlines of the island to indicate combat sorties. The name and the mission symbols painted on the aircraft are clearly visible in the crew photograph we took after returning to Hurlburt Field. (See Figure 21)

[Author's Note: The permanent name given to tail number 69-6575 during the Vietnam era of the 1970's was "Wicked Wanda," and that's the name you will find listed on several gunship oriented web sites. Our renaming her as the "Grenada Grinder" was very temporary for our Grenada mission only. Shortly after we returned and after our crew picture was taken at her parking spot on the Hurlburt flight line, our nose art quickly disappeared under freshly sprayed "gunship gray" paint at the direction of the Maintenance Officer. Under normal circumstances, gunships are not allowed to be decorated with nose art!]

O'CLUB WITH A-10 PILOTS

We flew our last mission over Grenada on the morning of 2 Nov 1983, and after stopping for fuel at Barbados on the way back, landed at Roosevelt Roads for the last time at 1240. We stopped by the Visiting Officer's Quarters to stow our luggage (not knowing where we might RON, we always took our luggage with us), and then the five officer crewmembers went to the Officer's Club (O'Club) for a little liquid refreshment. Our flight home to Hurlburt wasn't scheduled until 0800 the next morning so we had plenty of time to kill.

When we walked into the bar it was crowded with (young) A-10 Warthog pilots from England AFB, LA [1]. One immediately noticed our Spectre Gunship shoulder patch and called out to the others, "Hey, they're Spectre pukes!" Several rushed us as we walked to the bar and started asking questions in quick fire succession. We spent most of the afternoon telling war stories (and lies) and couldn't buy a libation for ourselves or them. A good time was had by all until we wished them well and departed for dinner and crew rest fairly early in the evening. (Yes, I said early).

They were a pretty good bunch but seriously ticked that they didn't get to play in the main event. These guys liked to shoot as much as we did. They were on their way to Barbados as our replacements, and would stand strip-alert at Barbados for several days should any firepower be required at Grenada.

RETURN FLIGHT TO HURLBURT

We departed Roosevelt Roads shortly before 0800 local time on November 3rd, and arrived back at Hurlburt at about 1230 local, logging 5.8 hours non-stop on a more direct route home. After clearing Customs at the aircraft and before we went to debrief maintenance, there was one last item of business to take care of at the airplane.

One of the things I really wanted to do before the crew dispersed for the last time was to get a picture of the whole bunch in front of our aircraft, now aptly named "Grenada Grinders", with a small outline of Grenada stenciled in white for each combat sortie we flew. This was the last chance to do that.

It was a proud moment for me and I hope for each of them. I'm very glad that we made the picture. This crew had performed exceptionally well, and flying with these professionals in a wartime scenario in harm's way was a real pleasure. I will always remember them and be thankful for their outstanding performance under fire and for our safe return home.

Figure 21 – The "Grenada Grinders" of Lima 56 after return to Hurlburt, 3 Nov 1983. Courtesy of Lt John Lasota. Front row, left to right: Lt Col Paul Wonderly, SSgt Roy Duncan, SSgt Bruce Grieshop, MSgt Luther Reece, SSgt Morris Blumenthal, TSgt Gary Carter, SSgt Roger Betterelli, SSgt John Eutzy. Back row, left to right: Lt George Williams, Maj Scott Stephens, Maj Michael Couvillon, TSgt Glenn Gaudette, Lt Col Robert Wenger, SSgt Larry Hickey, SSgt Bob Anderson, Capt Kirby Locklear, SSgt Chico Daleccio. Not pictured: Lt John Lasota.

NOTES - CHAPTER 3

AIRBORNE BATTLEFIELD COMMAND AND CONTROL CENTER (ABCCC)
1. *History of Tactical Air Command*, 276.
2. *History of Tactical Air Command*, 275.
3. Muirhead e-mail to recap telecon, 18 Apr 2007.
4. *Colonel Cox's Urgent Fury Trip Book*, 141.
5. Thigpen, *Praetorian Starship*, 282.
6. *History of the 2nd Air Division*, 134.
7. Thigpen, *Praetorian Starship*, 283.
8. *2nd Air Division After Action Report*, 15.
9. Adkin, *Urgent Fury*, 210.
10. *Colonel Cox's Urgent Fury Trip Book*, 141.
11. Morris e-mail, 23 Jun 2007.
12. Ibid.
13. Lima 57 (Sims) Mission Scenario.
14. Ibid.
15. Mahoney e-mail, 21 Apr 2007.
16. Sparks e-mail, 14 Jun 2007.
17. Ladd e-mail, 8 Jun 2007.
18. Ibid.

GRAND ANSE BEACH
1. Adkin, *Urgent Fury*, 269.
2. *2nd Air Division After Action Report*, 18.

UNCONTROLLED A-7S
1. Kemper e-mail, 6 Feb 2007.

MOVE TO ROOSEVELT ROADS
1. *2nd Air Division After Action Report*, 60.

O'CLUB WITH A-10 PILOTS
1. Playground Daily News, *Local Airmen End Mission in Caribbean*, 1.

CHAPTER 4
POST MISSION

INVITATION TO THE WHITE HOUSE

When I scanned the Playground Daily News before going to work on Friday morning, 4 Nov 1983, I saw an article about President Reagan's planned White House Ceremony. It was set for Monday, 7 Nov 1983, and four Hurlburt airmen would be attending. Of course my curiosity was immediately piqued as to who had been selected, so I went in to see Lt Col Fred Boyer, Deputy Operations Officer, just as soon as I arrived at the squadron.

"You're going, and you're leaving on Sunday", he said, and added, "Lt Col Jim Hobson from the 8th Special Operations Squadron and his radio operator, MSgt Howard Davis, are also going and traveling with you. Jim has your airline tickets. See you when you get back."

He also handed me an information sheet showing the required uniform of the day and the reporting time and place at the Pentagon. Unfortunately, the sheet also showed that the name of a fourth person, my lead gunner SSgt John Eutzy, had been scratched. I asked if there was anything we could do to get him put back on the list, because I thought his crew performance had been exceptional and he really deserved to go. I was assured that the slot was scratched at a higher command level, and had nothing to do with the person we had selected to go.

Fred explained further that all participating Air Force units had to be represented by a very small group of only 10 people, and we were only getting three slots. The same limit was being placed on each of the other services as well for a total of only 40 military attendees[1]. That was a low blow and I felt really bad about it for John, but there wasn't anything we could do about it.

POST MISSION

MEET AT THE PENTAGON

Lt Col Jim Hobson, MSgt Howard Davis, and I traveled by commercial air to Washington National Airport on Sunday morning, 6 Nov 1983, and stayed at the Crystal Gateway Marriott. On Monday morning we entered the Pentagon via the river entrance and reported at 0800 to the Protocol Office, 4th floor, E ring, 9th corridor, across from the Chief of Staff Office. After a brief welcoming ceremony, our protocol host served light refreshments as we chatted with our fellow Air Force participants and waited for our transportation to the White House.

After a few minutes, Air Force Lt Col James D. Woodall came up to me and introduced himself as an F-15 pilot assigned to the 33rd Tactical Fighter Wing at Eglin AFB, our neighbor base just across town from Hurlburt Field.[1] After he described the part he played in the mission, I recalled having seen their F-15s and AWACS aircraft parked on an inactive cross runway when we first landed at Roosevelt Roads on the 25th.

Of course none of us knew it at the time, but Lt Col Woodall and his F-15 buddies and an E-3A AWACs aircraft were either on strip alert or airborne on station somewhere between Cuba and Grenada.[2] The idea was to convince any insistent Cuban MIG-23 pilots that it was a bad idea to try to go to Grenada on a one-way trip to play with our U.S. forces. This also applied equally to interference with any aircraft on the route of flight to Grenada. The intervention was successful, none showed, and we were all very happy about that. Years later I heard (perhaps rumor) through another source that some did come up to play, but were "escorted" back to their base.[3]

ARRIVE AT THE WHITE HOUSE

Shortly after 0900 we were herded downstairs to our luxurious blue Air Force (school) bus. After a very enjoyable ride through Washington, we arrived at the White House and entered the grounds through the southwest pedestrian gate. We then walked up the circular driveway to the south lawn, just below the south portico where the reception was convening for a scheduled 1000 start.

As I walked up the circular driveway I noticed two very tall Army Ranger NCO's walking toward me and questioning each group ahead of me. They were wearing their green service uniforms with bloused trousers over highly-polished jump boots, their Ranger's tab and coveted Black Berets. The group just in front of me stopped when the Rangers questioned them, and they turned and pointed directly at me. Then they walked up to me, saluted smartly, and asked, "Sir, are you the gunship pilot?" I replied, "yes I was one of three," and they shook my hand strongly and said, "Major, you saved our butts! We were caught next to the runway (at Point Salines) without cover, and your gunfire stopped those SOB's dead in their tracks. We were certainly done for if you hadn't done that, and we can't thank you enough." (expletives deleted)

I told them that maybe it wasn't me and my crew in particular that had done it, but it could have been any of the three gunship crews that were there doing the job. After telling them that I was there representing all Spectre crewmembers, I assured them that I would be glad to pass their sentiments to my colleagues when I returned to the squadron at Hurlburt Field.

I'll never forget that moment. To be thanked for presumably saving the lives of fellow Americans and military members who were there with you in harm's way was one of the most gratifying and humbling experiences that I have ever had. That was B-I-G! That experience was the topping to a most enjoyable event that was to follow shortly.

WHITE HOUSE CEREMONY ON THE SOUTH LAWN

As we walked up to the south lawn of the White House, each of us were handed a commemorative (4"x 6") U.S. flag for waving. The front section of the seating area was reserved for students and military attendees. I sat next to a medical student named Sal Guarnera, a young man from Brooklyn, New York. We had a very enjoyable conversation while we waited, each briefly telling about our Grenada experiences.

The ceremony started at about 1045. President Reagan spoke[1] for a few minutes, and was followed by remarks from several student leaders who also presented him with a commemorative plaque as a token of their appreciation. Other dignitaries attending included Mrs. Reagan, Secretary of Defense Caspar Weinberger, Chairman of the JCS General John Vessey, congressional members, and other special VIPs and guests.

Figure 22. President Reagan speaks at the White House reception

When the speeches were all done, President Reagan filed through each row to shake hands and speak individually with each student and military attendee. He was closely followed by Secretary Weinberger and General Vessey. When it was my turn to speak to the President, I thanked him for having given us the opportunity to execute the mission and help to rescue our fellow Americans. What a thrill to shake hands and speak with the President!

Sal took several pictures before and during the ceremony and promised to send me selected copies. In late January 1984, as advertised, I received a very nice letter from him along with the promised photographs. The flag, his letter, and the three photos are a treasured testament to my attendance at that patriotic, heart warming, event.

When all the official festivities were done, we were escorted by aides on a White House tour that was specially arranged for students and military guests. About two hours later, the tour was completed and we returned to the Pentagon.

That was a once in a lifetime event. How many members of the military have had the opportunity to participate in a successful combat operation on behalf of the United States, and then visit the White House to be personally thanked by the Commander-in-Chief? For me that happened only five days short of my 20th year on active duty.

AIR FORCE TIMES INTERVIEW

After returning to the Protocol Office at the Pentagon, several of us were asked to interview with Air Force Times (AFT) for an article to appear in the 21 Nov 1983 issue. The interviewer was Mr. Leonard Famiglietti, an AFT staff writer, with photos by Mr. Jim Garamone, the staff photographer. My interview took less than 30 minutes and focused on a few highlights of the mission.

The other three Air Force members interviewed were the Combat Control Team commander from Pope AFB, NC, a Security Policeman from Little Rock AFB, AR, and a C-141 Loadmaster from Charleston AFB, SC.

Shortly after the interview was completed, Lt Col Hobson told me that we had to stick with our original return flight to Ft Walton Beach to be able to participate in a press conference scheduled for the next day, Tuesday, 8 Nov 1983. We quickly departed the Pentagon, grabbed our bags and checked out of the hotel, and made our 1650 flight through Atlanta, arriving home at 2100.

POST MISSION

As advertised, the interview with my picture appeared on the front page of the 21 Nov 1983 issue of AFT under the banner "4 Recount Roles in Grenada Action."[1] The caption next to my picture read, "Darkness was our friend. They could hear but not see us." The article continued on page four under the quote, "My Crew was First on the Scene" in large bold type.

HURLBURT PRESS CONFERENCE

The next order of business for Lt Col Hobson, MSgt Davis, and me was a press conference scheduled for Tuesday morning at 1000.

Before the Press Conference started we were told by high-level wing officials, "Now don't say anything specific…be intentionally vague. Tell them what you thought or how you felt, but don't talk about unit designations, specific times or tactics, or anything classified." What a big help that was! What else was there to say? I'm in trouble!

The press conference was 1,000 times worse than anything I have ever done before in my life. When combined with the distinct possibility of not being able to follow instructions and maybe revealing something classified, along with the heat and lights and dumb questions, that was no picnic! And judging from the stupid answers I gave that were printed in the newspaper the next day, I didn't do too well either.[1] Fortunately, Jim Hobson and Howard Davis took part of the heat so I didn't have to field every question. Was I ever glad when that was over!

Awards were passed out to all of the 1st Special Operations Wing's Grenada participants at the end of February 1984. My Air Medal award (6th Oak Leaf Cluster) was sent to me by U.S. mail in March because I was retiring from the Air Force and was on retirement leave on the day of the ceremony. I didn't find out about my second Air Medal award, 7th Oak Lead Cluster, until a week ago (3 Nov 2010) as I was wrapping up this book and preparing it for publication.

NOTES - CHAPTER 4

INVITATION TO THE WHITE HOUSE
1. Playground Daily News, *4 Airmen Expected to Meet President*, 1.

MEET AT THE PENTAGON
1. Playground Daily News, *Hurlburt, Eglin Men Attend Ceremony*, 1.
2. Adkin, *Urgent Fury*, 141.
3. Kemper e-mail, 6 Feb 2007.

WHITE HOUSE CEREMONY OF THE SOUTH LAWN

1. President Reagan's Speech at White House Ceremony, 7 Nov 1983

- http://www.reagan.utexas.edu/archives/speeches/1983/110783a.htm

AIR FORCE TIMES INTERVIEW
1. Air Force Times, 21 Nov 1983, *4 Recount Roles in Grenada*, 1.

HURLBURT PRESS CONFERENCE
1. Playground Daily News, 9 Nov 1983, *Pilots compliment Grenada students*, B1.

CHAPTER 5
MISSION SCENARIOS & TIME LINES: LIMA 57 THRU LIMA 61

LIMA 57 (SIMS) MISSION SCENARIO

Lima 57, commanded by Lt Col David Sims, was the second of three Operation Urgent Fury mission gunships to depart Hurlburt Field on 24 Oct 1983 bound for Grenada. Shortly after takeoff and while tweaking the guns over the Eglin range, number four engine caught fire. The aircraft made an emergency landing after extinguishing the fire and dumping fuel to reduce the aircraft weight. In minimum time the crew transferred to the spare aircraft, and departed again, only one hour and twelve minutes behind schedule. The route of flight to Grenada was the same as Lima 56 with two night heavyweight air refuelings enroute.[1]

Due to the late departure from Hurlburt, Lima 57 (Sims) received direction from ABCCC prior to arrival at Grenada to cancel the assigned Ft Rupert (aka Ft George) time on target (TOT), and instead proceed directly to the Point Salines Airport (PSA) to assist with the airfield seizure.[2] Upon arrival there he entered orbit at 6500 ft with Lima 56 (Couvillon) and Lima 58 (Twiford) already stacked in orbit at 6000 ft and 5500 ft respectively. Like the other two gunships already there, Lima 57 listened to the radio traffic with the Ranger FACs as they assigned targets. He searched with his TV and IR looking for enemy positions, and was configured in orbit and ready to arm a gun and shoot at any time.

While waiting for a turn to work a live fire target as directed by a Ranger FAC, the crew saw an Army Blackhawk helicopter crash on Amber Belaire Hill, a sparsely populated area on the next peninsula to the east about two miles from PSA. Lima 57 (Sims) moved its orbit to the crash site and vectored-in a search and rescue (SAR) helicopter that arrived after a few minutes to rope down defending ground forces. As other SAR ground forces were inserted and the wounded extracted, it was necessary for Lima 57 (Sims) to provide suppressive gunfire against the enemy troops that began advancing and firing on the crash site from the north.[3]

The crashed helicopter was from the 160th Aviation Battalion, the Night Stalkers, from Ft Campbell, KY, crewed by Capt Keith Lucas and CWO2 Paul Price. It had been heavily damaged as it tried to land the Delta Force and SEALs in the assault on Richmond Hill Prison near the city of St. George's. Capt Lucas plus three Rangers onboard were instantly killed by horrendous incoming AAA fire during their second attempt, and several more crewmembers and Rangers were wounded.[4]

Prior to returning to a PSA orbit, Lima 57 (Sims) was tasked by ABCCC to reconnoiter Calivigny Barracks, the Cuban built Grenadian cantonment located on the third peninsula to the east, approximately four miles from PSA. After a brief overhead orbit and search by onboard sensors, the crew reported no activity in or around the camp compound.[5]

After returning to PSA orbit, Lima 57 (Sims) provided reconnaissance and direct fire support for the Rangers as they secured the airport and began moving north and east. Initially the enemy was firing from positions in houses and bunkers up the hill and along the ridgeline to the north requiring precise gunship targeting to prevent friendly-fire mishaps. In one instance, friendlies who were pinned down in an exposed position on the airfield behind a truck were taking fire from a nearby house up the hill. The crew fired 40mm rounds to destroy the house, set it on fire and got secondary explosions, all without endangering the friendlies. The house burned for hours.[6]

A short while later, Lima 57 (Sims) joined Lima 56 (Couvillon) to fire on a bunker in the Cuban Headquarters compound called Little Havana. After a few rounds of 105mm each, an estimated 150-250 Cuban "workers" surrendered to the Rangers. Subsequently, after firing the 105mm with a delayed fuze in a different part of the compound, the ground party reported that the Cuban radio station had been knocked out.[7]

In another instance, the crew fired a 105mm round with the delayed fuze setting to knock out a dug-in enemy position beneath a house also in close proximity to friendlies. The round penetrated the house and detonated as advertised at the proper point underneath to kill the entrenched troops.[8]

About mid-afternoon, Lima 57 (Sims) was directed to again join Lima 56 (Couvillon), this time at Government House, the residence of Governor General Sir Paul Scoon located on Mt Weldale in the city of St. George's. A SEAL team needed help to protect Sir Paul Scoon and his family and staff against PRA troops on the residence grounds, and two BTR-60 armored personnel carriers (APC) parked at the outer gate. Lima 57 (Sims) destroyed one APC and the second quickly departed.[9]

Due to incompatible radios, the SEAL team was communicating indirectly with the gunship through a SEAL radio relay contact at the airport, then via Army VHF up to the gunship. Each time the PRA troops threatened through the wooded grounds, a call was made requesting immediate fire support.

After six hours on station, Lima 57 (Sims) reached Bingo fuel and was directed (by ABCCC) to refuel and rearm at Grantley Adams International Airport, Barbados, instead of proceeding to Roosevelt Roads, Puerto Rico, as previously briefed. There they found 40mm grenade rounds and unlinked 20mm rounds, both the wrong kind for the gunship and completely unusable. In spite of the non-availability of ammunition, Lima 57 refueled and departed for return to Grenada with their remaining 3000 rounds of 20mm, no 40mm rounds, and 40 rounds of 105mm.[10]

Upon return to the island, Lima 57 (Sims) was directed for the second time to Government House to push back advancing PRA troops. More AAA came up within the orbit that had to be dealt with, and again a menacing APC appeared at the front gate but scurried off after a few rounds of 20mm got his attention. Later they were called back for a third time to destroy the adjacent Prime Minister's residence that was being used by the PRA, which they did with 1200 rounds of 20mm. It was on fire when they departed.[11]

Table 5. Lima 57 (Sims) Mission Timeline

Time (Z)	Event
24/2329	Takeoff Hurlburt Field at gross weight of 170,000 lbs
25/0115	Emergency landing Hurlburt Field with #4 engine shutdown (fire)
0142	Takeoff Hurlburt Field in ground spare aircraft
Unknown	Air Refueling #1 (night) with KC-135 to 175,000 lbs gross weight
Unknown	Air Refueling #2 (night) with KC-135 to 175,000 lbs gross weight
1015	Orbit overhead Point Salines Airport (PSA) at 6500 ft AGL. On-call for TIC
1045	Vectored SAR to downed helo at Amber Belaire. Shot suppressing fire for SAR
1115	Armed recce of Calivigny Barracks and vicinity. No activity at compound
1215	Ranger CAS orbit at PSA. Destroyed house with 40mm, got secondary explosion
1330	Worked Little Havana workers' compound target with Lima 56 (Couvillon)
1400	Supported TIC with Rangers pinned down. Suppressed enemy fire w/40mm
1430	Joined Lima 56 (Couvillon) to protect SEALs at Government House
1515	Ranger TIC northeast of PSA. Put down marking round and drew white flag
1530	Hit houses northeast of PSA with enemy dug in under houses
1705	Landed as directed at Grantley Adams Intl AP, Barbados for fuel
1830	Takeoff Barbados and return to Grenada
1930	Supported SEALs at Government House. Kill 2 AAA sites and shot an APC
2015	Destroyed 3 APCs approaching to attack Rangers NE perimeter of PSA
2100	Directed to hit Prime Minister's house w/20mm. Shot 1200 rds and set afire
2235	Landed Roosevelt Roads. RON. Day-1 mission complete
26/2135	Takeoff Roosevelt Roads for Barbados
2340	Landed Grantley Adams International AP, Barbados. RON
27/2155	Takeoff Barbados. Capt Hockman now the Aircraft Commander.
2257	Fired on suspected snipers in vicinity of Calivigny Barracks
28/0416	Landed Grantley Adams International AP, Barbados
28 Oct–2 Nov	Six armed recce mission of six hours on-station. Notable events:
28 Oct	Supported friendlies taking sniper fire at Egmont Point near Cuban barracks
28 Oct	Vectored helo for MedEvac. TIC w/82 near sugar factory. Unknown KIAs

It should be noted here that as the day wore on, the protection of the Governor General's party became the top priority objective for all U.S. forces. [12] Each of the six gunships assisted at least once during their mission, and would spend an hour or so in orbit defending each time. Lima 57 (Sims) took the honors with the highest tally of three visits.

For the last encounter of the day, Lima 57 (Sims) caught three APCs making an end run around the eastern edge of the Point Salines Airport defenses. While the Rangers were firing mortars and recoilless rifles at the advancing armored vehicles, Lima 57 (Sims) fired several 105mm rounds to stop them dead in their tracks. In the opinion of the ground commanders, had that attack occurred earlier in the day before the perimeter defenses had been setup, and without the assistance of the gunship, they could have caused real trouble for the airfield defenders. [13]

Lima 57 departed after spending 8½ hours total on station and landed at Roosevelt Roads to remain overnight after a 28 hour crew day. By then they were also very, very close to total Winchester (i.e., out of ammunition) on all the guns. [14]

LIMA 58 (TWIFORD) MISSION SCENARIO

Lima 58, commanded by Major Clement Twiford, was the third of three Operation Urgent Fury mission gunships to depart Hurlburt Field on 24 Oct 1983 bound for Grenada. The route of flight was the same as for Lima 56 and Lima 57 with two night heavyweight air refuelings enroute. [1]

Lima 58 (Twiford) arrived overhead Point Salines Airport (PSA) a few minutes early to make good his assigned time-on-target (TOT) of 0500 local. Under the protection of darkness at 5500 ft, they established an orbital search pattern looking for troop movements or mass assemblies of troops or vehicles on and around the airport environment. The situation remained quiet. [2]

Shortly before the scheduled drop time of 0500, the Air Component Commander in ABCCC, Colonel Bruce Fister, slipped it by 30 minutes to 0530. Unfortunately this new time was near civil twilight, so the gunship began to lose darkness as a tactical advantage for concealment against the brightening sky.[3] On that day, morning civil twilight occurred at 0537, with sunrise at 0558. At 5500 feet above the ground, these times were several minutes earlier.

As the new drop time arrived and the stream of MC-130s and C-130s started their run-in from west to east, their world lit up with searchlights and tracers from small arms and 12.7mm AAA, mostly coming from the ridge line immediately to the north of the runway. Despite the heavy gunfire, the lead aircraft dropped his paratroopers and then made an abrupt descending right turn to safety out over the water. As numbers two and three aircraft approached their drop point, they aborted their airdrop and also turned right out over the water to avoid the hail of gunfire.[4] The airdrop stream had been stopped cold. The tracered AAA fire then turned on Twiford's gunship.[5]

The heavier stuff from nearby ZU-23 guns also began firing at Lima 58 (Twiford) and got his immediate attention as the early morning sky continued to brighten. For the next few minutes, Lima 58 (Twiford) focused on knocking out the 23mm guns as the most serious threat. He was still shooting at the 23mm guns when the 1st Battalion, 75th Infantry (Rangers) (1/75), Air Liaison Officer (ALO), call sign Delta 75, hit the ground and made the first call for fire support at 0538. Lima 58's Fire Control Officer, Lt Col Dick Dougherty, answered the call immediately.[6]

The stick of 42 Rangers from the lead aircraft had landed on the runway abeam the control tower. They were in exposed positions and were getting pounded as the gunfire from the ridge line now focused on them. After a few minutes more of working against the 23mm threat, Lima 58 (Twiford) began shooting his 20mm and 40mm into directed targets along the ridge line to suppress the enemy air defenses (SEAD)[7], and to allow the 1/75 troops to move forward to positions with at least some minimal protective cover.

Lima 58 (Twiford) continued to fire into enemy positions as the ALO called out the targets. Unfortunately, the Fire Control Officer was having trouble with a balky fire control computer, and had to constantly insert manual aiming corrections. The 105mm electrical firing circuit had failed and the gun was being fired manually using a lanyard.[8]

During the attempt to shoot the seventh 105mm round, the breech block cracked and the gun mis-fired.[9] At that point safety procedures dictated that the round be manually extracted and jettisoned. Normally if the aircraft was not over an unpopulated area suitable for jettisoning, the aircraft would have to depart the orbit to deal with the emergency.

In this case, however, since part of the orbit was overwater (i.e., in orbit over the PSA runway, the southern half is completely over water) there was no need to pull off the orbit, only to stop firing for a few minutes while the gunners executed the emergency checklist and cleared the struck round. Unfortunately, the unserviceable breech block put the gun out of service and not available for the remainder of the flight.[10]

[**Author's Note:** When the 105mm round was being extracted for jettisoning, someone on the crew transmitted that the aircraft was having gun problems and was departing the orbit (probably before they decided what they were going to do). Lima 56 (Couvillon) heard that transmission and turned immediately from its position near Calivigny Barracks to proceed to PSA, there entering orbit over the airfield to provide uninterrupted support for the Rangers by continuing to fire at the AAA. Whether Lima 58 (Twiford) actually pulled off the target for a few minutes is a point of disagreement since part of the orbit was over water and the round could be jettisoned there. It is uncontested, however, that Lima 58 (Twiford) did stop firing for a few minutes while the problem was cleared.]

After a few minutes, Lima 58 (Twiford) re-established geometry and continued to fire at the AAA until it was silenced. They continued working with the Ranger ALO and the FACs to fire on enemy pockets as the troops pursued them up the hill and over the ridgeline. Even with being hampered by fire control problems, the crew was able to continue providing accurate and effective firepower although using ammunition at a faster rate. Targets that were better suited to the 105mm were passed to the other gunship(s) stacked in a similar orbit.

The airdrops resumed shortly before 0600 when the remainder of the 1st Battalion jumped in. As each company of the battalion dropped and began moving up to take positions along the ridge to the north, or from the airport area to the north and east, their FACs called for and got Spectre support, some with fire mission requests and some for reconnaissance.

Many of these units had worked with AC-130's on exercises in the past and were fully aware of the gunship's "eye in the sky" protective reconnaissance capability. Both gunship TV and IR sensors could scan areas ahead of a unit's line of movement to provide advance information or call an alert warning on potential trouble spots. The airdrops continued until the last of the 2nd Battalion completed just after 0710.[11]

Before mid-day, Twiford and crew reached Bingo fuel and Winchester at about the same time, and decided it was time to take it to the barn. They departed for Roosevelt Roads, Puerto Rico, and after refueling there proceeded to Grantley Adams International Airport, Barbados, where their first day's mission ended.

THE TUNNER AWARD

For their exceptional performance the morning of 25 October 1983, Major Twiford and crew won the Air Force Association's *Lt Gen William A. Tunner Aircrew Award* for Military Airlift Command's Best Overall Aircrew for 1983. The award was presented at the AFA Annual Convention in September 1984 attended by Major Twiford (now retired). An excerpt from the award reads as follows: "The slow-moving AC-130H doesn't normally duel with AAA batteries, but with enemy rounds bursting all around them, Major Twiford's crew engaged four

ZU-23 guns and took them out with highly accurate fire from their 20-mm and 40-mm guns." [12]

[Author's Note: In the official gunship bible of "do's and don'ts", it says (paraphrased), "Do not duel with AAA." It seems appropriate here to tell a "gunship" joke that (like the old gorilla jokes) also ignores the dire situation with the fatal consequences that Clem and his crew found themselves. Question: "What do you do when four 23mm guns on the ground below have you in their sights in broad daylight and are ready to hose you?" Answer: "You shoot 'em with your 20's and 40's, of course!" The scary part is that what actually happened and the setup in the joke are the same.]

MISSION AT CALIVIGNY BARRACKS

While providing the 24/7 on-call fire support on the afternoon of 27 Oct 1983, Major Twiford's crew, now in a different aircraft with call sign Lima 61, were on duty over Grenada when the attack on Calivigny Barracks at Egmont was executed. They were to join A-7s from the carrier USS Independence, Army heavy artillery, and naval gunfire in softening up the area prior to the Ranger's air assault. [13]

After landing at PSA to pickup one of the 2nd Battalion, 75th Ranger FACs, the crew was directed to commence bombardment of the buildings and facilities within the compound area. The Army's 105mm battery was already firing from an area east of the end of the PSA runway when they departed. [14]

Upon arrival they rolled-in overhead Calivigny and started shooting the 15 to 20 corrugated roof buildings with two rounds of 105mm each, generally destroying what was reported to be a vital training area for the PRA troops. They got a small secondary explosion from one of the buildings. They didn't see any movement or other evidence that anybody was there. [15]

They could, however, see the impact of the Army's incoming 105mm rounds. Most were landing short with only a few making it to shore on the western edge of the peninsula, but none were reaching the compound. The Navy's destroyers never fired because their rules precluded firing with aircraft near the target area.[16]

At the prearranged time, the Blackhawk helicopters arrived with the 75th Rangers aboard. Lima 61 (Twiford) saw part of the landings, and observed the aftermath of the collisions when the chopper's blades apparently tangled with each other. About that time they were directed to fire into the surrounding ridge to suppress reported incoming ground fire.[17]

CALIVIGNY MILITARY BARRACKS EGMONT, GRENADA

SOVIET STYLE OBSTACLE COURSE

AAA SITE

FIRING RANGES

Figure 23. Calivigny Military Barracks (up is northwest)

The mission for Lima 61 over Calivigny was completed as tasked. As it turned out that was the second to last fire support mission for the gunships in Operation Urgent Fury, although they continued to provide 24/7 on-call fire support until the cessation of hostilities on the 2nd of November. The last fire mission occurred on the 28th.

THE RANGERS SAY THANK YOU

Prior to the attack of Calivigny Barracks on 27 Oct 1983, Major Clem Twiford's gunship (now call sign Lima 61) was directed to land at the Point Salines Airport to pickup an Army FAC that had all the planned details of the mission.[18]

As he landed to the east and rolled out down the runway, he saw a group of Rangers in bivouac on the south side of the runway, slightly past his mid-field left turnoff. The "business side" of his aircraft was facing to the north, however, and the protruding guns apparently went un-noticed by the Rangers as he cleared the runway. Since the gunship appears to be a normal "slick" C-130 when viewed from the right side as they were seeing it, except for the dark grey color, it didn't attract their attention.

A few minutes later, after he had picked up his Army FAC, he taxied back onto the runway and turned east to proceed toward a C-141 that was offloading on the eastern end of the runway. This was to be a heavy weight takeoff and the taxi-back allowed him to use the entire available runway. He turned around on the runway prior to the C-141's position and then taxied west a short distance down the runway to reduce the prop blast on the C-141 from his impending takeoff.

With the "guns" side now facing to the south, the same group of Rangers then recognized his aircraft as a gunship and spontaneously started standing up and pointing. As he applied full power for takeoff and the engine noise reached them, they rushed to the side of the runway, gave thumbs up, waved hands and arms, jumped up and down, and became instant cheerleaders as he started and continued his takeoff roll immediately in front of them. (You haven't lived until you've had a gunship takeoff in your face!)

These Rangers were apparently the same bunch that Twiford and his crew, and the other two gunships, had defended at H-Hour against the Cuban and PRA manned 12.7mm and 23mm guns. Those guns were looking down their throats when they were without defendable cover immediately after they airdropped on and beside the runway. Without the gunship support, the Ranger's light-casualty airport assault might have turned out significantly different.

This informal display of appreciation apparently had a lasting impact on Major Twiford's crew, and especially on Clem. When I interviewed him 23 years after it happened, he told me this story first, and how more than any other single event on this whole mission, this impromptu "thank you" from those Rangers made his day, and figuratively "made the buttons on his chest pop with pride." The pride (and possibly a small miracle) seemed to lift him up as he cleared the end of the runway. On that heavyweight takeoff he used every foot of available runway, and needed all the help he could muster to get airborne.[19]

Table 6. Lima 58 (Twiford) Mission Time Line

Time (Z)	Event
24/2334	Takeoff Hurlburt Field at Gross Weight of 170,000 lbs
Unknown	Air Refueling #1 (night) with KC-135 to 170,000 lbs
Unknown	Air Refueling #2 (night) with KC-135 to 175,000 lbs
25/0900	Arrived PSA orbit at 5500 ft AGL. Supported Ranger TIC
0915	Made radio contact with Lima 56 (Couvillon)
0930	Engaged and destroyed AAA firing on airdrop MC/C-130s
0930	Lima 56 observes tracered gunfire and 23mm airburst shooting at Twiford
0945	Reported they were departing orbit due to #6 gun problem
1115	Fired 20mm & 40mm on enemy position within 50 meters of friendlies
1200	Bingo fuel and Winchester 20mm & 40mm. Departed PSA for Puerto Rico
1310	Landed Roosevelt Roads, Puerto Rico. Refuel. No ammo available
1640	Takeoff Roosevelt Roads for Barbados
1846	Landed Grantley Adams Intl Airport, Barbados. Day-1 mission complete
26/1034	Takeoff Barbados for PSA. Landed Barbados at 26/1600
27/1830	Takeoff Barbados
1939	Landed PSA to pickup Army GLO
1955	Takeoff PSA for CAS 82abn Calivigny Barracks. Softened multiple targets
28/0135	Landed Barbados
29/0015	Takeoff Barbados for 6 hour armed recce over Grenada
29/0745	Landed Barbados
29 Oct–1 Nov	Three Armed Recce missions of six hours on-station

LIMA 59 (KEMPER) MISSION SCENARIO

Lima 59, commanded by Major Donald Kemper, was the fourth Operation Urgent Fury mission gunship to depart Hurlburt Field bound for Grenada. This aircraft was launched on the 25th in response to the unplanned continuing requirement for gunships, and in immediate response to the need for additional ammunition.[1]

Lima 59 (Kemper) proceeded to Grenada using the same route and flight profile as the preceding mission aircraft with two heavyweight air refuelings. Upon arrival, Kemper and crew were directed to support the SEALs at Government House, followed by direction to attack the Radio Free Grenada (RFG) station and enemy forces at Beausejour, a small coastal community about three miles north of St. George's. Their attack damaged the transmitting antenna and destroyed two vehicles.[2]

Subsequently they performed a directed water search for the missing SEAL party that was attempting to hook-up with U.S. naval forces west of the island. After three hours without success they terminated the mission and proceeded to Grantley Adams Airport, Barbados, for RON.[3]

On 27 Oct 1983, Lima 59 (Kemper) was supporting the 82d Abn near Frequente when PRA troops firing from a line of trees began to harass the U.S. forces. The gunship attacked the enemy positions by firing 20mm and 40mm rounds (as directed) up and down the tree line for almost an hour until the hostile firing stopped.[4]

Also on 27 Oct 1983, while Lima 59 (Kemper) was supporting 82d Abn troops on the Lance aux Epines peninsula (about one mile east of the airport) he again had orbit conflict with A-7s. This time the A-7s were working a target at Ruth Howard near the sugar mill and drive-in movie (both depicted on the "tourist" map). One of the A-7s in a flight of four mistakenly strafed friendlies at an 82d brigade headquarters command post, causing 17 casualties. In the midst of the ensuing chaos and confusion on the ground, the remainder of Lima 59's live fire support mission was cancelled.[5]

Table 7. Lima 59 (Kemper) Mission Time Line

Time (Z)	Event
25/1552	Takeoff Hurlburt Field at Gross Weight of 165,000 lbs
Unknown	Air Refueling #1 with KC-10 to 165,000 lbs
Unknown	Air Refueling #2 with KC-135 to 165,000 lbs
26/0030	Damaged Radio Free Grenada tower at Beausejour. Destroyed 2 vehicles
Unknown	Support SEALs protecting Sir Paul Scoon at Government House
0300 (estimated)	Conducted SAR for SEALs in waters vicinity of St. George's Bay and north
0615	Departed Grenada for Barbados
0650	Landed Barbados for RON
27 Oct-31 Oct	Four Armed Recce missions four or six hours on-station. Notable events:
27-Oct	Supported defenses at St. George Univ Med campus. Air refuel with KC-10
27-Oct	Support 82 Abn near Frequente using 20mm and 40mm
28-Oct	CAS at Calivigny Barracks. Hit positions near tip of Calivigny point
28-Oct	Support 82 Abn south end of Prickly Point peninsula. Orbit conflict w/A-7

LIMA 60 (STRELAU) MISSION SCENARIO

Maj Larry Strelau and crew arrived at Grantley Adams Airport, Barbados, as passengers on a MAC C-141 at mid-afternoon local on the 25th. The evolved plan was for them to take Couvillon's aircraft (69-6575) and fly as long a mission as possible with the residual ammunition and Twiford's full 105mm load. Couvillon gave them a full operations briefing on what to expect along with map annotations, ground FAC call signs, frequencies, etc. Other than the loss of the SATCOM and only minor discrepancies, the aircraft was fully mission capable for a second sortie.

To avoid possible confusion for local air traffic control, it was decided to keep the same Lima 56 tactical call sign that the aircraft used when it arrived. (Strelau would revert to his assigned Lima 60 tactical call sign on all his subsequent missions.)

After a quick tweak overwater nearby to check the fire control settings at 7000 ft, Lima 56 (Strelau) arrived in orbit over Grenada and was directed by ABCCC to Government House where enemy ground troops were again moving closer to the SEALs position. They were directed to destroy the remains of the unoccupied Prime Minister's nearby residence which they did with 100 rounds of 40mm that set it ablaze.[1]

A few minutes later, they fired 20mm on 15-20 enemy troops that were massing again near the Governor General's residence, and then used 20mm and 40mm to engage a small AAA and one APC.[2]

Attention shifted approximately one to two kilometers to the east for the next targets located in the Ft Frederick and Richmond Hill prison areas. Lima 56 (Strelau) was cleared to fire on all targets on the road running north from Ft Frederick. Using each gun as needed, they fired at suspected enemy positions. The last target was a AAA battery 200 meters north of Richmond Hill prison where dwindling loads of 40mm and 105mm hits got a secondary explosion and set the target ablaze.[3]

Table 8. Lima 60 (Strelau) Mission Timeline

Time (Z)	Event
25/1800	Departed Hurlburt Field as passengers on MAC C-141
2100	Arrived Grantley Adams Intl AP, Barbados
2230	Face to face handoff brief from Couvillon, and will use his aircraft (575)
26/0130	Takeoff Barbados for Grenada using Couvillon's call sign (LIMA 56)
0215	Blunted enemy attack on SEALs at Government House from 7000 ft AGL
0300	Destroyed two AAA positions and two APCs.
0330	Fired 100 rds 40 mm into Prime Minister's residence. Building burned
0445	Engaged targets on road running north from Ft Frederick.
0500	Engaged and destroyed AAA battery 200m north of Richmond Hill Prison
0725	Fired on enemy troops in Ft Frederick area
0835	Landed Grantley Adams Intl AP, Barbados
27 Oct-2 Nov	Five Armed Recce missions of six hours on-station. Notable events:
28 Oct	Provided CAS to friendlies taking sniper fire in Egmont Point area
28 Oct	Vector medevac helo for soldier w/broken back. CAS w/82 near sugar factory

LIMA 61 (TARPLEY) MISSION SCENARIO

Lima 61, commanded by Capt David Tarpley, the fifth Operation Urgent Fury mission gunship, departed Howard AB, Panama on 25 Oct bound for Grenada. The aircraft arrived Grenada after one heavyweight air refuel and completed the wet boresight (aka "tweak") procedure offshore.

The crew spent several hours trying to get oriented, but the totally inadequate maps they had been issued in Panama made that virtually impossible. Additionally, the inadequate mission briefing they received made tactical work with live fire unsafe.

Their SATCOM was also unusable and the INS and radar unreliable. They were unable to get assistance from other gunships through no fault of their own because they had not been briefed on special secure voice procedures in effect.[1]

At Bingo fuel, they retired to RON Barbados to fight another day. The ammunition load they brought in was critical for the mission birds for Day-2 the next morning.

Table 9. Lima 61 (Tarpley) Mission Timeline

Time (Z)	Event
25/2235	Takeoff Howard AB, Panama at Gross Weight of 173,000 lbs
Unknown	Air Refueling #1 with KC-135 to 173,000 lbs
26/0400	Arrived on-station Grenada wo/maps for tactical work. SATCOM unusable
0835	Landed Grantley Adams Intl AP, Barbados
27/Unknown	Takeoff Barbados for Grenada
2200	At Grand Anse beach, destroyed crashed Marine helo w/20 & 40 mm
28/0505	Landed Barbados

EPILOGUE

In support of Operation Urgent Fury, 16th Special Operations Squadron aircrews flew six AC-130H aircraft on 64 sorties for a total flying time of 367.1 hours, the most of any participating unit. Rounds expended as follows: 20mm – 61,300; 40mm – 2,000; and 105mm – 690.[1]

Statistics like these showing combat time and rounds fired are interesting, and they are important for historical purposes. For the gunship, however, there is a far better gauge to determine success, and that is "what did we do for our customer?" In our business, lives are at stake. If you do it right you get a cigar and an "attaboy," if not, the consequences can be horrendous and permanent.

We responded with accurate, overwhelming firepower to those who called for help, and had many more true believers in the weapon system when hostilities ceased. Most importantly, I can say without contradiction that in Grenada we knew where the friendlies were, and we fired where they directed and did them no harm! And we hope they will always remember us.

During my research I occasionally came across something nice that our customers (or their friends) said about us. Negative comments were nil. These kinds of comments were our success quotient:

1. Per Col L.C. Rush, Jr (USA), 1/75 Rangers, S3 Air during Grenada, "The real heroes, from my standpoint, besides the Rangers who were killed and wounded, were the AC-130 crews. As you recall, the initial drop was broken up and aborted because most of the aircraft veered off and did not drop. BG (then LTC) Wes Taylor was pinned down on the ground with his RTOs (i.e., the unit's backpack radio operators) and a few other Rangers. The AC-130s came in and smoked everything— literally I could see smoking debris in several locations when we hit the ground. When I finally dropped, the airfield was quiet. The AC-130s had decimated the Cubans in the vicinity of the airfield, including the Air Defense weapons and crews. There

were some skirmishes afterwards in the general area, but few if any on the airfield itself." [1]

2. USCINCLANT, Finding: "During the operation, the most valued fire support system was the AC-130 aircraft. One AC-130 was continually on station. The AC-130 was the most accurate short response fire support system available. For the Army it was the easiest system with which to coordinate and communicate. The requirement to "minimize damage and casualties" was also a key consideration. The ground force commanders picked an accurate system with which they were familiar and with which communications were the easiest." [2]

Figure 24. Left: Maj Gen Trobaugh, 82nd Airborne Division Commander, and right: Gen Vessey, Chairman of the JCS

3. When the island appeared to be secure and the AC-130H crews requested to redeploy, Maj Gen Edwin L. Trobaugh, 82nd Airborne Division Commander, delayed them. He told his joint task force staff that he would give up his offshore naval gunfire, his land-based artillery, and his helicopters before he would release the Spectres. He wanted their timely surveillance and instant accurate firepower on hand as long as there were enemy

soldiers unaccounted for. "The gunships are enough", he told his staff. [3]

4. Kind words about the gunship's performance from our own 23rd Air Force Commander, Maj Gen William J Mall, Jr. were not unexpected, but it was nice to hear them anyway. Talking about the 23mm AAA that was firing on the lead MC-130E when he was onboard, and the searchlights that illuminated his aircraft as it approached the drop zone, Gen Mall said, "At that moment the success of the mission was in doubt, but help was on the way in the formidable firepower of the AC-130 Spectre gunship." He continued, "We directed the AC-130s that were orbiting at a higher altitude into position. After one pass by the gunship, the anti-aircraft fire was extinguished and we began dropping troops again." And finally, in General Mall's view, "the deadly capability of the Gunships to direct overpowering fire at selective targets with surgical precision saved the entire operation." [4]

5. Col Hugh L. Hunter, 1st Special Operations Wing Commander, who flew as an observer aboard Lima 57, said in a (Ft Walton Beach) Daily News interview, "Our gunships saved the day. With the defenses that had been set up around the airport, without the gunships we would not have been able to suppress the fire and we (U.S. Forces) would have lost a whole lot [of] aircraft. To say our gunships saved the day would be an understatement." He later added, "The idea was not to destroy half the country, but to go in and surgically take out enemy targets. This was a rescue mission and the AC-130H was the perfect vehicle for it." [5]

THE WHITE HOUSE

WASHINGTON

November 30, 1983

Dear Colonel Hunter:

It was a special pleasure for me to welcome to the White House the students of St. George's University School of Medicine together with the U.S. Military heroes who rescued them from Grenada. I want you to know that I deeply appreciate the courage and patriotism that all of you showed under enemy fire on October 25. Americans everywhere are proud of our young people and our brave men in uniform. We're delighted to have you home!

Many thanks for the medallion. It's a perfect remembrance of your support, for which I am truly grateful.

Nancy joins me in sending you and the men of the 1st Special Operations Wing our best wishes for the future.

Sincerely,

Ronald Reagan

Colonel Hugh Hunter, USAF
Commander
1st Special Operations Wing
Hurlburt Field, Florida 32544

Figure 25. Letter to 1st SOW from President Reagan (copy of the original was distorted).

UNITED STATES AIR FORCE AWARDS FOR PERSONAL ACHIEVEMENT

"By direction of the President, each of the following is awarded the Air Medal for outstanding achievement while participating in aerial flight during the period indicated."

This quote is from Special Order G-581, dated 20 July 1984, which was issued by Headquarters Military Airlift Command (MAC) to recognize and reward the extraordinary efforts of Spectre Gunship aircrews during Operation Urgent Fury. Two Air Medals were actually awarded to each officer and airman, one for the combat action on 25 October 1983, and a second (Special Order G-15, dated 6 January 1984) for the inclusive period 26 October to 4 November 1983. A medal of higher precedence, the Distinguished Flying Cross (DFC) with "V" device for Valor, was awarded solely to Major Clement Twiford, the aircraft commander of Lima 58 for his heroic combat action over Point Salines Airport on 25 October 1983.

The citation that accompanied each award described the specifics of the individual accomplishments with typical statements such as "{rank & last name} contributed significantly to the success of the Grenadian rescue mission by providing massive and accurate close air support during the airdrop and airland of friendly forces onto Point Salines Airfield. In spite of intense antiaircraft artillery fire, {rank & last name} destroyed numerous enemy positions, including a ZU-23-2 anti-aircraft gun near the airfield." The citation closes with "The professional ability and outstanding aerial accomplishments of {rank & last name} reflect great credit upon himself and the United States Air Force."

EXPLANATION OF THE EARLY PROBLEMS WITH THE AWARD APPROVAL PROCESS

Soon after the Grenada mission was completed, the Wing Commander directed the preparation of the personal award packages based on the extraordinary level of accomplishment in the actual mission scenario. His initial determination was that the aircraft commander of each of the three crews that flew overhead the Point Salines Airport and defended the exposed Special Forces on the morning of 25 October 1983 would be recommended for the Silver Star (Awarded for distinguished gallantry in action against an enemy of the United States). Each member of their respective crews would be recommended for the DFC (Awarded for heroism or extraordinary achievement while participating in an aerial flight). The second award package for the Air Medal (Awarded for meritorious achievement while participating in aerial flight) was also recommended for the same crews but for the inclusive period 26 October to 4 November 1983. This is the way the two packages were prepared and submitted up the line to HQ MAC in late 1983.[6]

Unfortunately, the appropriate office at the Department of Defense (DoD) was flooded with award requests from the four participating services that reflected their intent to award too many and too high awards for what they (the DoD) thought was deserved. Consequently, the packages were downgraded as directed by DoD and resubmitted with the final package content as described above in the actual awards. It was reported to be a sore subject up the chain that the Wing Commander could do nothing about.[7]

The key issue here was the downgraded award's effect, not only for peer recognition, but more importantly to the officer or airman's career. Citations that accompanied all awards become part of the officer or airman's permanent personnel record, and an award of higher precedence (e.g., DFC or Silver Star) could notably increase the officer or airman's probability for promotion, his selection for professional military education schools, and even his choice of assignments. In short the higher ranked awards were appropriate for this mission and were expected; it was a *__BIG__* deal they were not awarded!

The following list shows the Order of Precedence and Weighted Airman Promoted System Point (WAPS) Value of the following Air Force Ribbons: 5th – Silver Star (9); 8th – Distinguished Flying Cross (7); 10th – Bronze Star (5); and 14th – Air Medal (3). [8] WAPS Values are used in computing promotion points for Air Force enlisted personnel competing for a higher grade. So the award of a higher precedence medal versus a lower one makes a significant difference.

GRENADA GRINDER

In my opinion, it was unconscionable for a high ranking officer(s) or high-level DoD bureaucrat(s) in the Pentagon to deprive these Special Operations officers and airmen of their justly deserved recognition because the level and/or number of recommended awards "just didn't look good." Their frivolous decision made a travesty of the DoD Military Awards Program.

Looking at the Special Order that actually awards the Air Medal to the individuals, you can quickly see by the number of Oak Leaf Clusters (OLC) these mid-career NCO Spectre crewmembers already had, that although it counted for WAPS points, another Air Medal had virtually no effect as a real reward or for peer recognition.

GUNSHIPS OLD AND NEW

Two retired AC-130A gunships are on static display in the Fort Walton Beach area, one (53-3129) at the Air Armament Museum near Eglin AFB, and the second (56-0509) at the Hurlburt Field Memorial Air Park. Others are proudly on display at museums here and there, not the least of which (54-1630) is at the National Museum of the United States Air Force at Wright-Patterson AFB, OH. The old A-models had an analog fire control system and were the first AC-130's to see service in Southeast Asia in the 1970's. There are no retired H-models on static display.

Today in October 2010, eight AC-130H Spectre gunships remain in the active duty Air Force inventory and are operated by the 16th Special Operations Squadron, now at Cannon AFB, NM. Seventeen of the new AC-130U Spooky gunships have been recently acquired, and are operated by the 4th Special Operations Squadron, Hurlburt Field, FL.

From what I read in the newspapers and see on the news, the aircrews of both the old and new systems continue to make history and create legends of their own in Iraq and Afghanistan. But they continue to do it the old fashioned way, by supporting and protecting the ground troops with accurate, overwhelming firepower.

PILOT IS OUT OF THE SIGHT
SAFE THE GUN!

NOTES - CHAPTER 5

LIMA 57 (SIMS) MISSION SCENARIO

1. *2nd Air Division After Action Report*, 21.
2. *History of 2nd Air Division*, 130.
3. *History of 2nd Air Division*, 139.
4. Adkin, *Urgent Fury*, 189.
5. *History of 2nd Air Division*, 139.
6. Ibid.
7. Ibid.
8. Ibid.
9. Ibid., 138.
10. Ibid., 140.
11. Ibid.
12. Kukielski, *Grenada: Five Years Later*, A-12.
13. *History of 2nd Air Division*, 140.
14. Ibid., 143.

LIMA 58 (TWIFORD) MISSION SCENARIO

1. *Colonel Cox's Urgent Fury Trip Book*, 99.
2. Twiford e-mail, 3 Dec 2006.
3. Ibid.
4. Ibid.
5. Ibid.
6. Roper, *Aardvark & Rangers*, 238.
7. Ibid., 239.
8. Broyles telecon, 29 May 2007.
9. Ibid.
10. Ibid.
11. Adkins, *Urgent Fury*, 210.
12. Lasyone, *The Navigator*, 7.
13. McMichael, *Urgent Fury: Looking Back*, 11.
14. Schmitt interview, 24 Jan 2007.
15. Ibid.
16. McMichael, *Urgent Fury: Looking Back*, 11
17. Schmitt interview, 24 Jan 2007.
18. Twiford telecon, 2 Dec 2006.
19. Ibid.

LIMA 59 (KEMPER) MISSION SCENARIO

1. Diggins e-mail, 24 Feb 2007.

2. *History of 2nd Air Division*, 141.
3. Ibid.
4. Kemper e-mail, 6 Feb 2007.
5. Ibid.

LIMA 60 (STRELAU) MISSION SCENARIO
1. *2nd Air Division After Action Report*, 19.
2. Ibid.
3. Ibid.

LIMA 61 (TARPLEY) MISSION SCENARIO
1. *2nd Air Division After Action Report*, 24.

EPILOGUE
1. Quote in email from Col L.C. Rush, Jr (USA), (1/75 Rangers, S3 Air during Grenada) to
Tom Greer. 25 Sep 2008
2. USCINCLANT, *Joint Overview of Operation Urgent Fury*, 1 May 1985, 7
3. Zeybel, *Gunships at Grenada*, 56
4. The Commando, *General Mall on Grenada*, 2 Dec 1983
5. *Playground Daily News*, 6 November 1983, 1
6. Colonel David Sims, former 16th SOS Commander, email 11 Nov 2010, Re: Awards and Decs for Grenada?
7. Ibid.
8. *Air Force Ribbons and Medals*, http://usmilitary.about.com/od/airforcemedals/l/blafmedals.htm (accessed 16 Nov 2010)

APPENDICES

APPENDIX A
AC-130H GUNSHIP PRIMER

Figure 26. The guns of the AC-130H are shown in this photo. #1 and #2 20mm guns are forward of the wheel well fairing (just forward of the propeller shadow), #5 40mm gun is in front of the APQ-150 radome (just aft of the wing shadow), and the #6 105mm gun with its red flash suppressor protrudes aft of the radome. (This picture was taken during the KC-10/AC-130H air refueling compatibility test at Edwards AFB, CA, in 1981. Note the crew entrance door is installed for this non-tactical mission.)

CREW OPERATIONS

Crew Size - The minimum crew size for tactical operations is 14. Extra crewmembers called augmentees (i.e., Pilot, Navigator, Flight Engineer, and Illuminator Operator), raise the total to 18 and increase the allowable crew day on extended missions. (The crew day limit during Operation Urgent Fury was waived.) Up to seven extra crewmembers are sometimes carried on local training flights. The limiting factor is the total number of seats available to strap in for takeoff and landing.

Personal Equipment - All crewmembers must wear flame retardant flight suits, boots, gloves, and an inflatable underarm life preserver if overwater operation is anticipated. On combat missions, crewmembers additionally wear survival vest with weapon and holster, parachute harness (with chest chute detached but located nearby), and ballistic helmet. Oxygen masks must be connected and available next to each crew position for immediate use, or worn continuously if cabin altitude exceeds 10,000 feet. The AC-130H cabin is un-pressurized.

Use of Checklists - Virtually all phases of gunship operation are setup using crew checklists. A particular checklist is called for by the pilot, and is used to configure for a specific activity. The checklist is read aloud on the interphone with each appropriate crew position responding for items in their area of responsibility. Titles of typical checklist for basic aircraft operation include, for example, before starting engines, before takeoff, and before landing. Titles of typical checklists for tactical operation include pre-strike and post-strike. Although not specifically mentioned in the detailed narrative, the reader may assume that all operations were performed in accordance with the required checklists, governing regulations, and approved operating procedures.

AIRCRAFT SYSTEMS AND OPERATION

Air Refueling - The AC-130H is capable of air-to-air refueling as are most of the other Special Operations MC-130 and EC-130 aircraft. These aircraft have additional fuel system plumbing and an external air refueling receptacle located above the cockpit to allow the airborne transfer of fuel from KC-135 or KC-10 tanker aircraft. Once the rendezvous is made with the tanker, a normal onload process is completed in approximately 30 minutes. Special training is required for the pilots, flight engineer, and navigator to be air refueling qualified. For the receiver pilot, air refueling demands delicate flight control movements and precise airspeed control to stay on the boom within the position envelope.

Aircraft Gross Weight - Normal peacetime C-130 maximum allowable gross weight is 155,000 lbs. Under certain circumstances, such as emergencies or wartime missions, commanders may authorize operations up to 175,000 lbs. For the Grenada missions in Operation Urgent Fury, the gunships were authorized to operate up to 175,000 lbs. Significant challenges in reduced aircraft performance were expected and handled, especially in the areas of initial takeoff and air refueling operations.

Interphone Systems - Three interphone systems are used to conduct crew communications. The Main Interphone is used by the cockpit crew for normal flight related communications. Private 1 (P1) is used by the Flight Engineer, Lead Gunner and his gun crew. Private 2 (P2) is used by the fire control team (i.e., navigator, fire control officer, TV and IR sensor operators, and the electronic warfare officer) during tactical operations. The two pilots and the navigator monitor radios being used on air traffic control or air refueling frequencies, and the fire control team monitors the radios being used to talk to ground parties on tactical frequencies.

Radio Equipment - AC-130's have a variety of onboard radio systems for talking to the appropriate agency during all phases of operations. The list includes: UHF radios for communicating with air traffic control, tanker aircraft or other mission aircraft (all air force aircraft must also monitor "Guard" channel on 243.0 MHz at all times); VHF radios mostly used to talk with civilian control towers; HF radios for long-range communications while on extended overwater flights; and FM for talking with Army ground control parties. A somewhat recent addition to the gunship was the UHF Satellite radio (SATCOM) that enabled direct communications via satellite repeaters with distant command agencies or other aircraft. The antenna for this system was mounted externally on the center escape hatch and sometimes didn't work well when the aircraft was in the bank associated with orbit geometry.

Pylon Turn - The gunship flies a left-hand pylon turn at altitude with the target at ground center. For each selected altitude there is an airspeed and a bank angle, called "nominals", where the target's relative ground position will remain fixed with respect to the orbiting gunship. These nominal values are used by the fire control computer to generate gun depression and lag angles to aim each gun so that a round fired while on nominals (excluding gun errors, system errors, and ballistic wind) will impact the target.

When the gunship is flying exactly on the prescribed imaginary orbit in the sky and is holding the required nominals (i.e., altitude, airspeed and bank angle), the condition is called "on geometry" or "on nominals." Normally while on geometry the autopilot is "on" to control the elevator servo to maintain altitude. The aileron servo is "off" so that the pilot can manually control the ailerons as required to increase or decrease bank angle to stay on orbit. Similarly, the rudder servo is also "off" so that the pilot can trim the rudder to maintain a coordinated turn. The copilot adjusts the throttles as necessary to maintain nominal airspeed.

FIRE CONTROL AND GUN SYSTEMS

Ammunition - The combat load is 3000 20mm, 400 40mm, and 100 105mm. The 40mm and 105mm rounds are stored in special racks located in the rear of the aircraft near their respective guns. The 20mm rounds are stored in their delivery containers until they are linked and "hung" in their feeder cans adjacent to the guns located up front. When carried, extra 20mm and 40mm ammunition is stored in their delivery cans and is tied down at selected floor locations.

Firing Mode, Fixed - In the fixed firing mode, the gun depression angle and the gun lag angle is fixed to nominal values and the fire control computer makes aiming adjustments based on those values. The pilot must adjust the aircraft bank angle to move the computed impact point to coincide with the target symbol. When preset computer parameters are satisfied and the pilot presses the trigger button, the gun fires.

Firing Mode, Trainable - In the trainable firing mode, the fire control computer moves the gun to track the target on its hydraulic gun mount and it is continually ready to fire. The pilot keeps his trigger pressed and adjusts his bank angle to stay on the firing orbit. The primary sensor operator actually fires the gun when he is satisfied with the aim and his consent button is pressed. Only the 40mm and 105mm guns have trainable gun mounts.

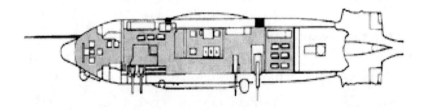

Figure 27. This drawing of the AC-130H shows the compartment locations of the side mounted guns.

Guns - The AC-130H has four guns: 2 each 20mm cannons mounted on the left side in the front of the cargo compartment; 1 each 40mm Bofors gun mounted on the left side just aft of the wheel well bulkhead; and 1 each 105mm Howitzer mounted on the left side just aft of the 40mm gun. (#3 and #4 guns were 7.62mm mini-guns, and had been removed because they were too small to be effective.)

Gun Safety System - Gunships have two systems that provide safeties to prevent an accidental firing. The first is the three arm/ safety (select) switches connected in series that are controlled by the Flight Engineer (FE), the Fire Control Officer, and the Lead Gunner. All three switches must simultaneously be in the "armed" position for the gun to fire. The second is the "fire enable" signal from the fire control computer, and switches controlled by the Fire Control Officer, the selected primary sensor operator (i.e., TV or IR), and the Pilot. When all preset computer limitations are satisfied, and all consent switches are "fire enabled" and the gun "Master Arm" switch is armed last by the FE, the gun will fire when pilot presses the trigger button.

Heads-Up Display (HUD) - Located to the pilot's left, the HUD allows the pilot to see the computer generated aiming imagery and geometry information while also visually seeing the target during the day (at night, the pilot only can only see the computer generated imagery). In simple terms, when the pilot superimposes the target symbol and the projected gun aiming point symbol by increasing or decreasing the bank angle, and then presses (with his left thumb) the trigger button on the yoke to fire the selected gun, the round will hit the target. Other symbology in the HUD assists the pilot with command bank-angle guidance to maintain or re-establish geometry.

Sensor, TV - The Low-Light Level Television (LLLTV or TV) sensor is mounted on a gyroscopic stabilized platform in the normal C-130 crew entrance door opening. It provides target azimuth and elevation to the fire control computer, and its television picture is visible at virtually all light levels both day and night. The field-of-view of the TV is partially limited at the extreme azimuth and elevation angles due to line-of-sight interference with the opening.

Sensor, IR - The Infrared (IR) ball sensor is mounted on a gyroscopic stabilized platform in the forward part of the left wheel well fairing. It provides target azimuth and elevation to the fire control computer, and its picture is generated based on differential infrared intensity values. The field-of-view of the IR is greater than the TV, and the IR can see straight down, and partially to the rear and outside the orbit.

Tweak - The commonly used term to represent the use of the wet boresight procedure to quantify the miss errors due to gun system anomalies and surface-to-altitude ballistic winds. By firing rounds at a target on selected headings around the firing orbit and entering the resulting miss distances, the fire control computer quantifies and stores the gun errors and applies the correction to the aiming point of subsequent rounds. This correction is referred to as the "gun delta", and is calculated for each gun. Likewise, the computer calculates the effects of the wind on the miss distance and direction, and applies the "ballistic wind" to the aiming point of each subsequent round. The tweak is normally performed before reaching the combat area.

TYPICAL TARGET ATTACK SCENARIO

Tasks by Crew Position:

Pilot – The pilot controls the airplane from the gunship's left seat and commands the attack.

FCO – The Fire Control Officer (FCO) operates the Fire Control (FC) computer and manages the fire control team (i.e., pilots, FCO, NAV, TV, IR, and EWO) on P2.

NAV – The crew Navigator guides the crew to the target area and confirms target locations and proximity to friendly forces.

FE – The flight engineer relays specific gun elements of the attack between the pilot and gun crew on P1.

TV/IR – Sensor operators search for and track targets under the direction of the NAV and FCO.

AG – The lead gunner and gun crew load and maintain the guns, and communicate with the FE on P1.

Gun Designations: #1 – 20mm, #2 – 20mm, #3 – 7.62mm (removed), #4 – 7.62mm (removed), #5 – 40mm, #6 – 105mm.

Step-by-Step Firing Preparation Sequence (Items 1 thru 13):

1. **FCO** – "Pilot, TV is tracking an enemy building at 4 miles, turn left to a heading of 030."

2. **Pilot** – "Turning left to 030. FCO give me TV guidance."

3. **Pilot** – "FCO, give me #6 gun, fixed. Navigator, any ground threats near the target?"

4. **FCO** – "Crew, TV is primary, #6 gun, Fixed. FCO is ready."

5. **NAV** – "NAV confirms the target. Pilot you are cleared to fire. No threats briefed for this area.""

INFO – The TV has been selected as the primary sensor, so the TV sensor operator must continuously track the selected target and turn his firing consent "ON."

INFO – FCO selects the desired gun (#6) in the Fire Control (FC) computer causing the gun's electronic position sensors for lag angle, depression angle, and the round's ballistic characteristics to be fed into the FC computer. The FC computer then uses these values along with the orbit parameters of airspeed, bank angle, aircraft altitude, and predetermined values for ballistic winds and gun pointing errors, to solve its program equations to generate visual aiming symbology for the pilot's Heads-Up (HUD) display.

6. **FE** – "Guns, make ready #6 gun, fixed mode." (FE sets #6 gun switch "ON")

7. **AG** – "#6 gun is ready." (AG loads the gun and sets #6 gun switch "ON")

8. **FE** – "Pilot, #6 gun is ready."

INFO – The pilot flies to the target using the Fire Control computer guidance that is displayed on his flight instruments. The guidance will align the aircraft to a tangent of the orbit and put it in position to roll into the orbit when abeam the target. As the pilot rolls-into the orbit, he commands the selected gun to be armed and visually transitions to the HUD on his left. In addition to the aiming symbology, the HUD displays orbit guidance to assist the pilot with acquiring and maintaining the firing orbit. Aircraft altitude is maintained by the autopilot with only the elevator servo engaged, and the copilot adjusts the engine power to maintain the selected nominal airspeed. The copilot and navigator monitor the radios for communications to/from any supported ground party.

9. **Pilot** – "Pilot is in the sight, arm the gun."

10. **FE** – "#6 gun is armed and ready" (FE moves the Master Arm switch to "ARMED")

INFO – When the pilot acquires the target in the HUD, and overlays the target symbol (i.e., the FC computer generated diamond symbol that identifies the target) with the computed impact point (i.e., the FC computer generated circular symbol that marks the computed point of impact), and stabilizes the aircraft to satisfy the aiming symbol's movement rate and coincidence values, and presses the trigger button under his left thumb on the yoke, **the selected gun will fire!** (A very slight 'bump' is felt in the cockpit when the #6 gun fires.)

INFO – As the attack continues, the pilot will direct the FCO to make any FC changes he may desire. The FCO will direct the TV and IR sensors as necessary to track this target or move to another target. The NAV will coordinate with the FCO to approve the selected targets, and will generally maintain crew awareness of mission requirements. Through the FE, the pilot will direct any desired changes on round type, or for #6 gun (the 105mm only) he can direct the lead gunner to manually set a fuze delay of .05 seconds which may make the round more effective against a hard target.

Figure 28. This gun crew loads an AC-130U's 105mm (same as for the AC-130H). The team's lead gunner (upper left) opens the 105mm breech to eject the spent shell, the 2nd gunner (lower right) removes the spent shell, and the 3rd gunner (upper right) inserts a fuzed round. The frame attached to the rear of the gun is the "safety cage" that protects the crew from the recoil. When the round is loaded, the lead gunner will close the breech, move the #6 gun switch to "armed," and call "gun ready" on the interphone.

INFO – If multiple rounds are required from the #6 gun, the gunners will quickly eject the spent shell, load the hot round and each time call the gun "ready", approximately every 5-10 seconds (more or less). When the FE hears the gunner's call, he arms the gun and announces "Gun ready." The pilot will then aim and fire when ready. Between rounds the pilot will maneuver the aircraft to maintain firing orbit and be ready to fire again when the gun is called ready. The primary sensor will report to the crew each round's impact result as either a "direct hit" or the miss distances in 'mils' (e.g., one high, one aft in milliradians) The FCO may enter these results into the FC computer to further 'tweak' the aiming solution.

11. **TV** – "Pilot, direct hit, target is burning and is destroyed!"

12. **Pilot** – "Pilot is out of the sight, safe the gun."

13. **FE** – "The gun is safe" (FE moves the Master Arm switch to "SAFE")

Firing sequence is complete!

APPENDIX B
AC-130H SPECTRE AIRCREW LIST FOR GRENADA

Tail No. Crew Position		69-6575 Lima 56	69-6574 Lima 57	69-6573 Lima 58	69-6569 Lima 59	69-6575 Lima 60	69-6567 Lima 61
Aircraft Commander	FP	Maj Couvillon, M J	*Lt Col Sims, D K	Maj Twiford, C W	Maj Kemper, D W	Maj Strelau, L H	Capt. Tarpley, D A
First Pilot	FP	Lt Col Wenger, R K	Capt Dieffenderfer, J C	Capt Waylett, T W	Capt Byers, M B	Capt Payne, S M	1Lt Britt, W J
Co-Pilot	CP	Maj Stephens, J S	1Lt Traster, R K	1Lt Phelan, M P	Capt Weathers, W W	1Lt Keltz, M A	2Lt Hoesen JD
Navigator	NAV	Capt Locklear, K R	Capt Broyles, B H	Capt Lasyone, B A	Lt Col Wurstner, R D	Capt Hamilton, M J	Capt Gallagher, T J
Navigator	NAV	1Lt Lasora, J A	2Lt Gavin, M R	2Lt Schmitt, R W	2Lt Crisafi, M L	2Lt Lee, Timothy	Maj Collette A E
Fire Control Officer	FCO	Lt Col Wonderly, P C	Maj Rudolph, R J	Lt Col Dougherty, R P	Maj Koerceuw, R I	Maj Bennes, J M	Lt Col Singleton, P L
Electronic Warfare Officer	EWO	1Lt Williams, G F	Capt Haren, K A	1Lt Neal, S F	Maj MacInnis, W H	Lt Col Turbiville, H P	1Lt Pijma, R F
Flight Engineer	FE	TSgt Gaudette, G J	CMSgt Eller, S E	CMSgt Beardsley, D L	MSgt Adkins, L G	MSgt Faulkner, D E	SSgt Rummage, D M
Flight Engineer	FE	SSgt Daleccio, F E	SSgt Sapp, S B	MSgt Hosenbacker, M J	TSgt Parchment, E W	TSgt Spencer, D A	TSgt Stone G D
LLLTV Sensor Operator	TV	MSgt Reece, L D	TSgt Kerwin, W J	TSgt Andersen, J L	TSgt Knight, M V	SSgt Vanstee, R D	MSgt Hollyfield, J J
IR Sensor Operator	IR	SSgt Anderson, R L	SMSgt Boudreaux, D	TSgt Sexton, A G	TSgt Buege, P G	TSgt McClintock, D A	TSgt Taylor, F O
Illuminator Operator	IO	TSgt Carter, G D	CMSgt Denoi, A G	MSgt Allen, W S	TSgt Humphrey, H J	TSgt Perez-Morales, C A	SMSgt Hall, R L
Illuminator Operator	IO	SSgt Duncan, R S	SSgt Hinderer, V B	SSgt Jennings, W L	SSgt McCarthy, M K	SSgt Pearson, A C	MSgt Gowdy C C
Lead Aerial Gunner	AG	SSgt Eutzy, J W	SMSgt Hays, D C	MSgt Broyles, R E	MSgt Cosens, B D	MSgt Gross, B G	MSgt West, J E
Aerial Gunner	AG	TSgt Hickey, L D	SSgt Colvin, D A	TSgt Smith, R K	TSgt Bupp, L L	SSgt Daniel, R L	SSgt Bonn, K J
Aerial Gunner	AG	SSgt Betterelli, R A	SSgt Lofgren, M J	SSgt Habas, J G	SSgt Skinner, D W	SSgt Rodriguez, S	SSgt Drummond, J P
Aerial Gunner	AG	SSgt Grieshop, B H	SSgt Pakutinski, A G	SSgt Celis, G G	SSgt Smith, C M	SSgt Hatch, T J	SSgt Bricker, D G
Auxiliary Crewmember	ACM	SSgt Blumenthal, M C	SSgt Mills, L T	SSgt Thompson, H L	SSgt Powers, S D	SSgt Hicks, S W	SSgt Walter, W B
			Col Hunter, H L				2Lt Franco V J (Nav)
			*Capt Hockman, R W				

*Hockman sub for Sims after 27 Oct 1983

APPENDIX C
AC-130H FIRING WITH EXTERNAL FUEL TANKS

All of the AC-130H Spectre gunship airframes were originally delivered to the Air Force as standard 1969-model Lockheed C-130E Hercules (69-6567 to 69-6577) [1]. Several years later the gunship package was added to the airframes, and the aircraft electrical, pneumatic, hydraulic, and other systems modified to create pseudo H-models. The major change was the form-fit-function upgrade from the Rolls-Royce/Allison T56A-7 engines to the more powerful T56A-15 engines, a change that was necessary to handle the added operating weight of the weapon systems.

The standard C-130E fuel tank configuration retained by the gunship includes six internal wing tanks containing a total of 6700-gallons of fuel, and two standard 1360-gallon under-wing pylon external fuel tanks mounted between the engines. The external tanks have two fuel pumps each and can feed any engine or transfer fuel during ground or flight operations. The external tanks and pylons are not air or ground jettisonable, but are ground removable. The later addition of the in-flight refueling capability did not affect the physical configuration or operation of the internal or external tanks.

Prior to 1981, the gunships were operated on live fire operational or training missions with the external fuel tanks removed to preclude possible tank, pylon, or wing mount damage from gun-blast overpressure when the left-side mounted guns fired. If additional fuel was necessary for deployments, the tanks would be reinstalled for in-flight use, and then removed at the destination before firing. The obvious limitation to this plan is the inability to deploy with tanks installed and then safely fire immediately upon arrival in the target area.

While this configuration limitation was thought to be necessary for safe operation, an assumption fully supported by both operations and maintenance, it had never been verified through actual measurement or analysis. It was believed that either the wing mount, pylon, or tank would be immediately damaged in the short term, or the cumulative effects of long term use would damage these components to the point of requiring constant repairs or replacement. No real data was available to support either position.

Finally in 1980, at the direction of HQ Tactical Air Command[2], the Air Force contracted with the Lockheed-Georgia Co. through the Warner Robins Air Logistics Center (WR-ALC) to study the problem through actual flight tests, and to issue a report with findings and recommendations[3]. Fortunately, because of my engineering background, extensive C-130 experience, and position as squadron Chief Pilot, I was selected to participate in the test as Aircraft Commander and Test Director. In addition to the flight crew, the test team consisted of two Lockheed-Georgia C-130 structural engineers who would analyze and study the data and write the report, and selected engineers from the 3246th Test Wing at Eglin AFB who would install strain gauges on all structures on the left wing. WR-ALC was tasked to provide a flight-rated test engineer to operate the in-flight recording systems for collecting the data.

Working with the Lockheed-Georgia engineers, the test team designed flight profiles to provide test points to evaluate gun blast effects throughout the operational and tactical flight envelope. The test points varied altitude, airspeed, and bank angles to produce gun depression angles and lag angles that generated overpressures from the least stressful case to the worst case for each gun. The test was flown in six sorties over a 42 day period in Apr-May 1981, and after local data reduction by the Test Wing at Eglin's Math Lab, the data was forwarded to Lockheed-Georgia in Marietta, GA for analysis.

The test produced exciting results in terms of reducing or eliminating the previously perceived firing hazards. The bottom line of the results was there was no danger of immediate damage from gunfire to the tank, pylon, or wing mount over the short term. This was confirmed by post-test NDI inspections on these test components[4]. Over the long term, if the tanks remained installed for repeated day-to-day operations, restrictions may be required only at certain #6 gun (105mm) lag angles associated with firing at the higher altitudes. No damage whatsoever was anticipated from firing the #1 or #2 gun (20mm), or the #5 gun (40mm). In all cases, data confirmed no likely damage to the wing structure itself or engines from the gunfire.

These most favorable results translated into a "quick look" preliminary opinion issued by the structural engineers that there should be "no restrictions to firing with external tanks installed on a temporary basis." The finding would later be validated and permanently incorporated into the gunship's flight manual and tactical crew operations documents by complete removal of the previous firing restrictions so as to be in effect prior to October 1983.

Next time you see pictures of any AC-130H gunship operating in Grenada, you will see that the external tanks were installed. The extra fuel available in-flight from these extra tanks (approximately three hours total) was the direct reason that the gunship could deploy from the continental United States, fly non-stop to Grenada with two air refuelings enroute, fire upon arrival as required, and stay on-station for hours more before leaving to air refuel again. The combat operations over Grenada marked the first time combat application of the AC-130H gunship firing unrestricted with the external fuel tanks installed.

APPENDIX D
AIR REFUELING FROM THE KC-10

Prior to May 1981 the only Air Force air-to-air refueling tanker available for fixed wing aircraft use was the Boeing KC-135 Stratotanker. During that month the KC-10/AC-130H Receiver Qualification Test was flown at Edwards AFB, CA, as part of the KC-10's Initial Operational Test and Evaluation (IOT&E) phase. Based on the success of this test, all air refuelable C-130's were cleared to use the KC-10 on training and operational missions without restriction.

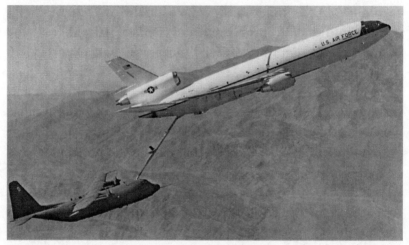

Figure 29. The first KC-10-to-C-130 air refueling during IOT&E. (The tilted camera has distorted the climb angle to appear steeper than normal)

The AC-130H gunship was the only C-130 receiver used in this portion of the KC-10's IOT&E. At that time only Special Operations C-130's, namely the AC-130H Spectre, the MC-130E Talon, and the EC-130E ABCCC were air refuel capable. Of the three, the AC-130H, with a Drag Index of +83 (and even higher with IR protective engine exhaust "tubs" installed), was the worst case because it had the highest drag index and was the heaviest over its operational weight envelope. If this tanker-receiver combination was successful as a test case, then all other C-130's should be operationally air refuel viable.

On 3 May 1981, the 1st Special Operations Wing, 16th Special Operations Squadron, provided an AC-130H gunship with a minimal non-tactical crew to Edwards AFB as tasked by Tactical Air Command (TAC) to participate in the IOT&E. I was on orders as the Aircraft Commander and Instructor Pilot (IP). Over the following seven days we flew over 26 hours on 9 sorties to test the tanker-receiver capability. The assigned Flight Test pilot, Lt Col Bob Black, flew the left side pilot's seat and I flew the right seat.[1]

During each sortie we evaluated factors such as aerodynamic capabilities and limitations, tanker boom and fuel systems compatibilities and problems, and tanker navigational and boom/director lighting. Special note was taken of KC-10 differences or peculiarities, especially any hazards that may have been discovered. Our takeoff fuel weight and the in-flight fuel onload were closely managed to assure that all gross weights were tested. During the latter sorties I took pictures of what the refueling picture looked like to the pilot in the pre-contact and contact positions as well at the extremes of the boom envelope. Although C-130s were subsequently approved for unrestricted refueling from the KC-10, there were two significant findings that needed to be passed along via pilot familiarization briefings.

First, higher power settings were required to overcome the tanker generated turbulence and "bad air", the term we coined to represent the downwash and vortices that were far more severe than from the KC-135. For the power-limited gunship this meant that the only way to stay on the boom at the higher gross weights was to request the tanker "toboggan" at 200-300 feet per minute (fpm). This technique slightly reduced the power required and made station keeping and maneuvering possible. For this test the maximum allowable normal C-130 gross weight of 155,000 lbs was mandatory.

Second, the KC-10 is so large that it filled the wind screen and made the pilot feel like he was always too close and needed to back out to get back in position. The opportunity to establish good visual alignment clues to maintain the center of the envelope was essential and the preflight familiarization made possible with the pictures I took made this a lot easier

Over the next several weeks I had the opportunity to brief and fly with the Standardization-Evaluation pilots and squadron IP's of both the 7th ACCS flying EC-130E's from Keesler AFB, MS, and the 8th SOS flying the MC-130E's from Hurlburt Field. Both checkouts consisted of the ground briefing followed by a day/night air-fueling sortie with the KC-10.

The second part of the mission follow-up was to draft part of the KC-10/C-130 Receiver Qualification Test Report for the Test Pilot, Lt Col Black. This included all of our operational evaluations and favorable/unfavorable factors that would contribute to the determination of feasibility for this air refueling combination.

On the morning of 25 Oct 1983, the gunship had another operational "first" with an air refueling with the KC-10 under combat conditions. After I had been on station over Grenada for several hours, we got down to "Bingo" fuel and called for the stand-by KC-10 tanker. During this refueling I had the opportunity to explore aircraft performance up to the higher gross weight of 170,000 lbs but just couldn't "pack" any more fuel in. Legally, I could have gone up to the Emergency War Plan allowable of 175,000 lbs.

I was absolutely ecstatic that I already had the previous KC-10 experience and this was not my first time. It was like old home week, but under a far more trying circumstance!

APPENDIX E
EC-130E AIRBORNE BATTLEFIELD
COMMAND & CONTROL CENTER (ABCCC)

The EC-130E ABCCC aircraft were assigned to the 7th Airborne Command and Control Squadron (ACCS), a Tactical Air Command asset at the time of Grenada, and based at Keesler AFB, MS, also the home of the WC-130 "Hurricane Hunters" of the 53rd Weather Reconnaissance Squadron (WRS). The ABCCC aircraft were specially modified to carry a 40 ft. "capsule" that snugly fit into the aircraft's cargo compartment containing working areas and seating for 15 battle staff members, a galley, and latrine facilities.

The capsule was equipped with every type of radio and communications equipment possible to permit each battle staff member to talk with dedicated air and ground assets on UHF, VHF, and FM, and for worldwide communications on HF, SATCOM, and teletype. With the exception of the two "Mickey Mouse" ears heat exchanger pods for the air conditioners mounted high on the fuselage forward of the wings, and the wing-tip probe antennas and additional blade antennas on the fuselage top and bottom, the EC-130E looked like every other C-130 (see Figure 16). The other barely noticeable exception is that like the Special Operations MC-130 and AC-130 aircraft, the ABCCC aircraft were equipped with the air-to-air refueling modification, giving it virtually unlimited airborne endurance and range. Also like the gunships, all of aircraft had been modified with the more powerful T56 Dash-15 engines to replace the standard C-130E T56 Dash-7 engines.[1]

The ABCCC flight crew complement of five was consistent with the standard C-130 crew positions, and the flight deck was virtually unchanged. The ABCCC Battle Staff in the capsule had 12 members working in four functional areas: command (2), operations (3), intelligence (2), and communications (5). The capsule could seat 15 persons, thus allowing for seating up to three extra user command element members (like the

JSOC command element on the Grenada mission) as dictated by mission requirements.[2]

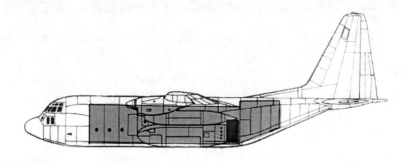

Figure 30.   The ABCCC capsule fits snugly into the C-130 cargo compartment.

The 42nd ACCS, successor to 7th ACCS, under the command of Lt Col Norm Potter was deactivated at Davis-Monthan AFB, AZ, on 30 Sep 2002 after 34 years of service, having been involved in every large military operation from Vietnam to Kosovo.[3] The ABCCC command and control function was assumed by the more modern E-3 Airborne Warning and Control System (AWACS) and the E-8 Joint Surveillance Target Attack Radar System (Joint STARS) aircraft.

Although having flown thousands of hours each over a 40 year period, most of the squadron's aircraft were transferred to other C-130 units and are still actively flying missions today. These airframes were highly desirable because, unlike the normal airlift C-130s, they all have the air-refueling modification installed. In 2002, three were scheduled to be converted into the HC-130P variant to fly with the several Combat Search and Rescue (CSAR) units assigned that mission. Two airframes, 62-1818 and 62-1825, were found to be un-serviceable and were retired to AMARC (bone yard) at Davis-Monthan AFB, AZ. Aircraft 62-1809 was lost at Desert One during the Iran hostage rescue.[4]

In 1968 I briefly flew the ABCCC mission from Udorn AB, Thailand. At the time I was assigned as a C-130E Instructor Pilot with the 314th Tactical Airlift Wing, 345th Tactical Airlift

Squadron, at Ching Chuan Kang AB, Taiwan. The 12-hour plus missions flew racetrack orbits over southern Laos. At least one of the four missions, call signs Hillsboro, Cricket, Moonbeam, or Alley Cat, was on station 24/7, and was the primary operational control agency for all the fast movers going up to North Vietnam.

An ABCCC capsule is on permanent display at the Air Force Armament Museum located near the Main Gate at Eglin AFB, FL. The museum is open 7 days a week except for federal holidays, and there is no admission charge. (Visit the museum's web site for driving directions and more information.)

[Author's Disclaimer: The ABCCC Aircrew List in Appendix F may not be 100% accurate. It was constructed from the 25-year old recollection of several of the individuals who flew the missions. Unfortunately, none of the crewmembers had an actual copy of their Crew Orders in their personal papers. So no one had a real good handle on exactly who flew with whom, and agreement on the final list was accepted as a consensus.]

Figure 31. Looking aft in the ABCCC static display capsule

APPENDIX F
ABCCC AIRCREW LISTS FOR GRENADA

Crew Position	1st Aircraft (62-1825)	2nd Aircraft (62-1818)	3rd Aircraft (62-1857)
Aircraft Commander	Lt Col James Williams	Capt Jack Carkeet	Capt Mike Mahoney
First Pilot	Capt Brian Muirhead	Capt David Clutts	
Co-Pilot	Lt Mike Morris	Capt Greg Brewer	Capt Todd McClimans
Navigator	Capt Mike Conn	Lt Roger Hall	Lt Dale Mack
Flight Engineer	TSgt Harold Norwood SSgt Norm Morrissette	TSgt Winfield Scott	SMSgt Rich Kletecka
Detachment Commander (DETCO)		Lt Col John Dalton	
Director of Airborne Battle Staff (DABS)	Lt Col Dick Breslin	Major Kenneth Fields	Lt Col George Balog
Battle Staff Operations Officer (BSOO)	Major William K. Esterly	Major Larry Barbee	Capt Robert Warner
Airborne Weapons Controller (AWC)	Capt Gerry Kesseler	Capt Eric Morin	Lt Johnny Hinson
Airborne Aircraft Controller (AAC)	TSgt Larry Bishop	TSgt Donald Watkins	TSgt Robert Schmidt TSgt David Spurlock
Airborne Intelligence Officer (AIO)	Lt Mark Kellinger	Capt Aubrey McEachern	Capt Keith Hinton
Airborne Intelligence Technician (AIT)	SSgt Ken Miller	SSgt Mike Walker	Sgt Ken Sparks
Airborne Communication System Operator (ACSO)	MSgt Len Winston SSgt Joe Poore	TSgt Ruben Quero TSgt Gerald Hopkins	MSgt Mike Sullivan TSgt Steve Ladd
Airborne Maintenance Technician (AMT) / Scanner	SSgt Brian Garner SSgt Colin Chalmers	MSgt Eddie Driggers SRA Jim Bedard	SSgt Mac Kyles
Joint Task Force 123 / Commander	MGen Richard Scholtes		
Joint Task Force 123 / Deputy Commander		Colonel Palmer	
Air Component Commander (ACC)	Colonel Bruce Fister		
Deputy Air Component Commander (ACC)		Lt Col Jim Schenk	

NOTE: Crew lists shown above are typical only. Crewmembers were not assigned to specific hard crews for all flights. Individuals were rotated between crews or substituted as required to cover exigencies.

Alternate: Major Hugh McCormick
Crewmembers: Capt Gene Whitten, Lt Bill Stoops, Maj Gibson

NOTES - APPENDICES

AC-130H FIRING WITH EXTERNAL FUEL TANKS
1. *1969 Serial Numbers*, Lockheed C-130E 69-6567 to 69-6577.
2. HQ TAC/DOR, *AC-130 Weapons Certification*.
3. Lockheed-Georgia Co., *AC-130H External Fuel Tank Combat Certification*. Report.
4. Poe, *Non-Destructive Inspection (NDI) of AC-130 Test Tank and Pylon*.

AIR REFUELING FROM THE KC-10
1._ Lt Col Black was promoted to O-6 and later assigned to Eglin AFB as the Air Armament Center Deputy Commander. After his retirement a few years later, Col Black served as the military liaison to Mr. Joe Scarborough, the U.S. Congressional Representative from Northwest Florida. As of this writing in May 2009 he is the Military Representative on the Florida Staff of Congressman Jeff Miller.

EC-130E AIRBORNE BATTLEFIELD COMMAND AND CONTROL CENTER
1. globalsecurity.org, *EC-130E ABCCC Aircraft*.
2. Ibid.
3. Ibid.
4. Roddy email, 4 Jul 2007.

GLOSSARY

82d Abn	82nd Airborne Division
A-7	Navy attack aircraft
AAA	antiaircraft artillery
ABCCC	EC-130E Airborne Battlefield Command and Control Center
AC	Aircraft commander
ACCS	Airborne Command and Control Squadron
AD	air division (or ADIV)
AFA	Air Force Association
AFROTC	Air Force Reserve Officer Training Corps
AFSOB	Air Force Special Operations Base
AFT	Air Force Times
AFTO 781	Aircraft maintenance status forms
AG	aerial gunner
AGL	altitude above ground level
aka	also know as
ALCE	airlift control element
ALO	air liaison officer
AP	Associated Press
APC	armored personnel carrier
API	Armor piercing incendiary
API-T	Armor piercing incendiary tracer
AR	air refuel
ARCP	air refuel control point (geographical point in latitude/longitude)
ARCT	air refuel control time (time in Zulu)
ATA	actual time of arrival
ATC	air traffic control
ATD	actual time of departure
AWACS	E-3A Airborne Warning and Control System

Bingo	fuel on board required to recover at base including required reserves
CARP	computed air release point (for airdrops)
CAS	close air support
CCK	Ching Chuan Kang AB, Taiwan
CEOI	Communications and Electronics Operating Instruction
CG	aircraft center of gravity
CIP	computed impact point (where the bullets will hit)
CP	command post or copilot
DCS	deputy chief of staff
DD Form 175	military flight plan form
DIA	Defense Intelligence Agency
DMA	Defense Mapping Agency
DZ	drop zone
ETA	estimated time of arrival
ETD	estimated time of departure
ETE	estimated time enroute
EWO	AC-130H Electronic Warfare Officer (pronounced e-wo)
EWP	Emergency War Plan
FAA	Federal Aviation Administration
FAC	Forward air controller (ground or air)
FCO	AC-130H Fire Control Officer (pronounced fo-co)
FE	flight engineer
FIR	Flight Information Region
FM	frequency modulated aircraft communications radio
Form F	aircraft weight and balance form (DD Form 365F)
FP	first pilot
GLO	Army Ground Liaison Officer
HEI-T	High explosive incendiary tracer

helo	helicopter
HQ	headquarters
HUD	AC-130H pilot's heads up display (on pilot's left)
INTEL	Intelligence, J2
IOT&E	Initial operations test and evaluation
IP	instructor pilot
IO	illuminator operator (current designation is now LM – Loadmaster)
IR	AC-130H gunship's infrared sensor
JCS	Joint Chiefs of Staff
JSOC	Joint Special Operations Command
JTF	joint task force
KIA	killed in action
Km	kilometer
MAC	Military Airlift Command
medevac	medical evacuation helicopter
MSL	altitude above mean sea level
NAV	navigator
NM	nautical miles
NSC	National Security Council
NSDD	National Security Decision Directive
OBE	overcome by events, superceded
OECS	Organization of Eastern Caribbean States
ops	operations
OSD	Office of the Secretary of Defense
PA	primary aimline (designates target in the HUD)
PRA	Grenadian People's Revolutionary Army
PRM	Grenadian People's Revolutionary Militia
PSA	Point Salines Airport
rds	rounds of ammunition
recce	armed reconnaissance

RMC	Grenadian Revolutionary Military Council
ROE	rules of engagement (limitations on attacking targets)
RON	remain overnight
RTB	return to base
SAR	search and rescue
SATCOM	satellite UHF communications radio
SEAD	suppression of enemy air defenses
SEALs	Navy Sea Air Land special warfare forces
SKE	C-130 formation station keeping equipment
SOS	Special Operations Squadron
SOW	Special Operations Wing
stick	A group of paratroopers jumping on the same DZ pass
TAC	Tactical Air Command
TAS	Tactical Airlift Squadron
TAW	Tactical Airlift Wing
TDY	temporary duty
TIC	troops in contact (within 1 kilometer of target)
toboggan	descent of 200-300 feet per minute while refueling
TOT	time on target
TTB	through-the-boom interphone communications
TV	AC-130H gunship's low-light level television sensor (LLLTV)
tweak	AC-130H wet boresight procedure to calculate aiming errors
UHF aircraft	ultra-high frequency, primary communications radio
UPT	Undergraduate Pilot Training
USA	United States Army

USAF	United States Air Force
USLANTCOM	U.S. Atlantic Command
VHF	very-high frequency, secondary aircraft communications radio
w/	with
wo/	without
Winchester	out of ammunition (or for a specific gun)
WR-ALC	Warner-Robins Air Logistics Center
WRSK	war readiness spares kit (maintenance)
Z (ZULU)	Greenwich mean time

BIBLIOGRAPHY

BOOKS

Adkin, Major Mark. *Urgent Fury: The Battle for Grenada.* Lexington, MA: Lexington Books, 1989.

Carney, Col John T. and Benjamin F. Schemmer. *No Room for Error: The Covert Operations of America's Special Tactics Units from Iran to Afghanistan.* New York: Random House Inc., 2002.

Cullen, Tony, and Christopher F. Foss, eds. *Jane's Land-Based Air Defence 1990-91.* 3rd Edition. Alexandria, VA, 1990.

Durant, Michael J. and Steven Hartov with LtCol Robert L. Johnson (USA, Ret.). *The Night Stalkers: Top Secret Missions of the U.S. Army's Special Operations Aviation Regiment.* New York: G.P. Putnam & Sons, Inc., 2006.

Gormly, Capt Robert A. (USN, Ret.). *Combat Swimmer: Memoirs of A Navy SEAL.* New York: Penguin Putnam Inc., 1999.

Harding, Stephen. *Air War Grenada.* Missoula, MT: Pictorial Histories Publishing Co., 1984.

Kallander, Dean C. and James K. Matthews. *Urgent Fury: The United States Air Force and the Grenada Operation* Scott Air Force Base, IL. Military Airlift Command Office of History Monograph. 1989.

O'Shaughnessy, Hugh. *Grenada: An Eyewitness Account of the U.S. Invasion and the Caribbean.* New York, Dodd, Mead, 1984.

Roper, Jim. *Aardvarks and Rangers.* Baltimore, MD: PublishAmerica, 2004.

Thigpen, Col Jerry L. Colonel (USAF Ret.). *The Praetorian Starship: The Untold Story of the Combat Talon.* Maxwell AFB AL: Air University Press, 2001.

Warnock, A. Timothy. *Short of War: Major USAF Contingency Operations, 1947-1997.* Maxwell AFB, AL: Air Force Historical Research Agency, 2000.

CLASSIFIED SOURCES

Headquarters Air Combat Command, ***History of the Tactical Air Command, 1 January – 31 December 1983, Volume I*** (Langley AFB VA). (Secret) Pages 269-280 (redacted), Urgent Fury, are now declassified.

Headquarter 2nd Air Division, ***History of the Second air Division, 1 July – 31 December 1983, Volume One Narrative,*** (Hurlburt Field, FL, 1984) (Secret) Section IV, pages 123-172 are now declassified.

DECLASSIFIED SOURCES

The White House, ***National Security Decision Directive 110, Grenada: Contingency Planning*** (Washington DC: National Security Council, October 21, 1983) Document formerly classified Top Secret is now declassified.

The White House*, **National Security Decision Directive 110A, Response to Caribbean Governments' Request to Restore Democracy in Grenada*** (Washington DC:National Security Council, October 23, 1983) Document formerly classified Top Secret is now declassified.

Headquarters 1st Special Operations Wing (MAC), ***Colonel Cox's Urgent Fury Trip Book*** (Hurlburt Field, FL, no date). Document formerly classified Secret is now declassified.

Headquarters 2nd Air Division (MAC), ***After Action Report – Urgent Fury*** (Hurlburt Field, FL, 9 Nov 1983). Document formerly classified Top Secret is now declassified.

Headquarters Military Airlift Command (MAC), Office of History *Urgent Fury: The United States Air Force and the Grenada Operation.* Dean C. Kallander and James K. Matthews, (Scott Air Force Base, IL, January 1988). Document formerly classified Secret is now declassified.

NEWSPAPERS

Phil Kukielski, "Grenada: Five years later, evidence of snafus grows", The Providence Sunday Journal, Providence RI, October 23, 1988.

"U.S. Marines heading for Grenada" (AP) Washington DC, Playground Daily News, October 22, 1983.

"Grenada accuses U.S. of concocting invasion excuse" (AP) Port-of-Spain, Trinidad, Playground Daily News, October 23, 1983, 8A.

"Caribbean leaders rap Grenada; radio warns of invasion" (AP) Port-of-Spain, Trinidad, Playground Daily News, October 24, 1983, 3B.

"U.S. Marines spotted on Caribbean Island; Grenada mission eyed" (AP) Bridgetown, Barbados, Playground Daily News, October 24, 1983.

DOCUMENTS

1969 Serial Numbers, USAAS-USAAC-USAAF-USAF Aircraft Serial Numbers--1908 to Present. http://www.joebaugher.com/usaf_serials/usafserials.html (accessed 9 Nov 2010)

AC-130H External Fuel Tank Combat Certification, Lockheed-Georgia Co., Marietta, GA. Contract # FO9603-80-G-0417. 16 May 1980.

AC-130H Spectre, AC-130U Spooky. Federation of American Scientist. Military Analysis Network, US Military Aircraft. http://www.fas.org/man/dod-101/sys/ac/ac-130.htm (accessed 9 Nov 2010).

AFSOC Instruction 11-202, Volume 10. *AC-130H Operations.* 1 July 1997.

http://www.fas.org/man/dod-101/sys/ac/docs/11020210.pdf (accessed 9 Nov 2010).

AFSOC Instruction 11-203, Volume 5. *AC-130H Configuration/ Mission Planning.* 1 July 1998. http://www.fas.org/man/ dod-101/sys/ac/docs/11020305.pdf (accessed 9 Nov 2010).

Anything, Anywhere, Anytime: An Illustrated History of the Military Airlift Command,

1941-1991. Scott AFB, IL, Headquarters, Military Airlift Command, 1991. Operation Urgent Fury: Grenada, pp 180-183.

Cole, Ronald H. *Operation Urgent Fury: The Planning and Execution of Joint Operations in Grenada, 12 October - 2 November 1983.* Washington, DC: Joint History Office, Office of the Chairman of the Joint Chiefs of Staff, 1997.

EC-130E ABCCC Aircraft. http://www.globalsecurity.org/ military/systems/aircraft/ec-130e-abccc.htm (accessed 9 Nov 2010)

Joint Military Operations Historical Collection. Chapter III: Operation Urgent Fury. Washington, DC: Joint History Office, Office of the Chairman of the Joint Chiefs of Staff, 1997.

Lind, William S. *The Grenada Operation: Report to the Congressional Military Reform Caucus.* Washington, DC: Military Reform Institute, 1984.

Poe, Capt Rodger B. HQ 1st SOW/MAM, letter 9 Jul 1981, to Maj Couvillon, 16th SOS/DOV. Subject: Non-Destructive Inspection (NDI) of AC-130 Test Tank and Pylon.

Rivard, David T. *Analysis of Operation Urgent Fury.* Maxwell AFB, AL: Air Command and Staff College, Air University, 1985.

Simmons, Maj J. Mike, *Operation Urgent Fury: Operational Art or a Strategy of Overwhelming Combat Power?* Fort Leavenworth, KS: US Army Command and General Staff College, 1994

Time Life Books. *Commando Operations - The New Face of War (Grenada)*. 1991

Grenada: Tales of Things Gone Wrong, 63-97.

U.S. Dept. of Defense. Grenada: October 25 to November 2, 1983. 1983.

U.S. Depts of State & Defense. *Grenada: A Preliminary Report*. 16 Dec 1983.

Walker, D.E. Capt, MAC AOS/DTP. *COMALF/URGENT FURY: An Interview with BGen R.B Patterson, Vice Comdr 21 AF*, 1984.

LETTER

Eagleburger, Lawrence S., Under Secretary of State for Political Affairs. Letter, January 9, 1984. To The Washington Times, Letters to the Editor.

MESSAGE

HQ TAC/DOR 212120Z Mar 80 to DIR MAT MGT, WR-ALC. Subject: *AC-130 Weapons Certification*.

PERIODICALS

Binder, L. James. *Grenada Post-Mortem: A 'Report' That Wasn't*. Army, vol. 34, no. 6, Jun 1984, 12-16.

Bolger, Daniel P. *Special Operations and the Grenada Campaign*. **Parameters, vol. 18, no. 4,** Dec 1988, 49-61.

D-Day in Grenada. TIME, November 7, 1983, 22-28

Eller, Gene. Command Master Sergeant, 1ˢᵗ Special Operations Wing, USAF. *Spectre.* Field Artillery Journal, vol 53, no. 2, March-April 1985, 13.

Grenada: A Preliminary Report. Washington DC: Dept of State and Dept of Defense, 16 Dec 1984.

Grenada: Special Report. Airman, Feb 1984, 37-42

McMichael, Major Scott R. *Urgent Fury: Looking Back and Looking Forward.* Field Artillery Journal, vol 53, no. 2, Mar-Apr 1985, 8-13.

Now to Make It Work, TIME., November 14, 1983, 18-24.

Special Report: The Battle for Grenada. Newsweek, Nov 7, 1983. 66-76.

Why the Surprise Move in Grenada-and What Next? U.S. News & World Report, Nov 7, 1983. 31-34.

Zeybel, LtCol Henry (USAF, Ret.). *Spectre.* National Defense, Oct 1983, 47-50.

Zeybel, Henry. *Gunships at Grenada.* National Defense, vol. 68, no. 395, Feb 1984, 53-56.

EMAIL COMMUNICATIONS

Adkin, Mark, Author, Urgent Fury: The Battle for Grenada.

Betterelli, MSgt Roger (USAF, Ret.) Couvillon Crew Aerial Gunner

Burruss, Lt Col Lewis H. "Bucky" (USA, Ret.) Deputy Commander, Special Forces Ops Delta

Collette, Maj Alban E. (USAF, Ret.). AC-130H Navigator and JSOC Mission Planner

Gaudette, MSgt Glenn (USAF, Ret.). Couvillon Crew Flight Engineer

Gavin, Col Milo (USAF, Ret.). Deputy Chief of Staff, US Special Operations Command

Gormley, Capt Robert A. (USN, Ret.). Commander, SEAL Team Six

Kemper, Maj Don (USAF, Ret.). AC-130H Aircraft Commander

Mitchell, CMSgt Francis R. (USAF, Ret.). Superintendent, 7th ACCS (ABCCC)

Roddy, Ray. Author of **Circles in the Sky** - The Secret War in Southeast Asia

Sims, Col David K. (USAF, Ret.). Former 16th SOS Sq Comdr, AC-130H Aircraft Commander

Twiford, Maj Clement W. (USAF, Ret.). AC-130H Aircraft Commander

IN-PERSON INTERVIEWS

Locklear, Lt Col Kirby R. (USAF, Ret.) Couvillon Crew Navigator, 14 Mar 2007

Schmitt, Lt Col Robb W. (USAF, Ret.) Twiford Crew Navigator, 24 Jan 2007

Singleton, Lt Col Paul L. (USAF, Ret) Tarpley Crew Fire Control Officer, 21 Feb 2007

Wenger, Lt Col Robert K. (USAF, Ret.) Couvillon Crew First Pilot, 18 Apr 2007

TELEPHONE INTERVIEWS

Betterelli, MSgt Roger A. (USAF, Ret.) Couvillon Crew Aerial Gunner, various dates in 2006 and 2007

Burruss, Lt Col Lewis H. "Bucky" (USA, Ret.) Deputy Commander, US Army Delta Force, on/about 12 May 2007

Broyles, TSgt Ron (USAF, Ret.) Twiford Crew Lead Aerial Gunner, 29 May 2007

Collette, Maj Alban E. (USAF, Ret.). Joint Special Operations Command, Spectre Gunship Operations Planner, 9 Mar 2007 [assigned to 16th Special Operations Squadron on temporary duty at JSOC]

Diggins, Lt Col Bill (USAF, Ret) Staff Officer, 2nd Air Division, Hurlburt Field, FL, 25 Feb 2007

Dougherty, Lt Col Richard P. (USAF, Ret.) Twiford Crew Fire Control Officer, 24 May 2007

Eller, CMSgt Sherman E. (USAF, Ret.). Sims' Crew Flight Engineer, 23 Apr 2007

Fister, Lt Gen Bruce (USAF, Ret.). Joint Special Operations Command, Deputy Director of Operations, Air Component Commander for Grenada (ABCCC), on/about 25 Apr 2007

Gavin, Colonel Milo (USAF) DCS, Special Operations Command, Macdill AFB, FL, 12 Apr 2007

Gormly, Capt Robert A. (USN, Ret.) Commander, SEAL Team Six for Urgent Fury, 29 May 2007

McEachern, Lt Col Aubrey (USAF, Ret) Intelligence Officer, ABCCC, 24 Apr 2007

Mitchell, CMSgt Francis R. (USAF, Ret.). Superintendent, 7th ACCS (ABCCC), 24 Apr 2007

Robertson, Colonel "Robbie" (USAF, Ret.) Commander, AC-130H Maintenance Support Team at Barbados, 17 Apr 2007

Roper, Colonel James (USAF, Ret.) 1st Battalion, 75th Infantry (Rangers), AF Air Liaison Officer, 9 Feb 2007

Schenk, Lt Col Jim (USAF, Ret.) Joint Special Operations Command Senior Staff Officer for Urgent Fury, 22 Apr 2007

Terry, LtCol William R. (USAF, Ret.) Operations Officer, 16th Special Operations Squadron, 23 Apr 2007

Twiford, Maj Clement W. (USAF, Ret.) AC-130H Aircraft Commander, on/about 2 Dec 2006

PHOTOGRAPHS

C17902-6, President Reagan Briefs Congressional Leaders (accessed 9 Nov 2010). http://www.reagan.utexas.edu/archives/photographs/large/c17902-6.jpg

C18148-8, President Reagan speaks at White House Ceremony (accessed 9 Nov 2010). http://www.reagan.utexas.edu/archives/photographs/large/C18148-8.jpg

SPEECHES

Remarks at a White House Ceremony for Medical Students and United States Military Personnel From Grenada - http://www.reagan.utexas.edu/archives/speeches/1983/110783a.htm (accessed 9 Nov 2010)

INDEX

(The page numbers for the text content of the tables are not reflected in the Index page lists)

P

R

V

W

Z

ANY TIME ANY PLACE

1ST SPECIAL OPERATIONS WING

CPSIA information can be obtained at www.ICGtesting.com
Printed in the USA
LVOW13s1141300314

379527LV00005B/432/P